P9-DIF-738

World Book's

SCIENCE
& NATURE
GUIDES

ROCKS &
MINERALS

OF THE WORLD

World Book, Inc.
a Scott Fetzer company
Chicago

REF
J508
WOR

This edition published in the United States of America by
World Book, Inc., Chicago.

WORLD BOOK and the GLOBE DEVICE are registered trademarks or trademarks of
World Book, Inc.

World Book, Inc.
233 North Michigan Avenue
Chicago, IL 60601 USA

For information about other World Book publications, visit our Web site
http://www.worldbook.com or call **1-800-WORLDBK**
(967-5325). For information about sales to schools and libraries, call **1-800-975-3250**
(United States); 1-800-837-5365 (Canada).

Copyright © 2007, 2005 Anova Books Company Ltd.
151 Freston Road, London W10 6TH, United Kingdom
www.anovabooks.com

All rights reserved. No part of this publication may be reproduced, stored in a
retrieval system, or transmitted in any form or by any means electronic, mechanical,
photocopying, recording, or otherwise, without the prior written permission of the
copyright owner.

The Library of Congress has cataloged an earlier edition of this title as follows:

Rocks & minerals of the world.
      p. cm. — (World Book's science & nature guides)
      "Edited text and captions based on An illustrated guide to rocks
and minerals by Michael O'Donoghue"—T.p. verso.
      Includes bibliographical references and index.
      ISBN 0-7166-4217-4 — ISBN 0-7166-4208-5 (set)
      1. Rocks--Juvenile literature. 2. Minerals--Juvenile literature. Title: Rocks and
minerals of the world. II. O'Donoghue, Michael. Illustrated guide to rocks &
minerals. III. World Book, Inc. IV. Series.
QE432.2 .R645 2005
552—dc22
                            2004043464

This edition: ISBN 13: 978-0-7166-4229-9 ISBN 10: 0-7166-4229-8
ISBN 13 (set): 978-0-7166-4221-3 ISBN 10 (set): 0-7166-4221-2

The author and publishers would like to thank Dr. Joel Arem and
Dr. Wendell E. Wilson for loaning the majority of the photographs illustrating this
book.

© 1993 Wendell W. Wilson: 37BR, BL, 48, 49TL, BL, 48TR, BR, 49 TR, BL, BR, 50TL, B,
51TR, BL, BR, 52TL, BL, BR, 53TL, TR, 54, 55TR, B, 56TR, BL, 57T, 60, 61T, 62B, 63B,
64TL, TR, 65T, 67TL, B, 68TL, B, 69TR, BL, 70TR, 71TR, B, 72TL, BL, 73TR, BR, 74TR,
75,

© 1993 Joel Arem: 13-19, 20, 24-5, 28-33, 36-7, 40-1, 47TR, BR, 48TL, BL, 49TL
50TR, 51TL, 52TR, 53BL, BR, 55TL, 56TL, BR, 57B, 61B, 62T, 63T, 64BL, 65B, 66, 67TL,
68TR, 69TL, BR, 70TL,B, 71TL, 72TR, BR, 73TL, BL, 74TL, BL, BR.

By courtesy of Natural History Museum, London: pages 20/21, 27/27.
By courtesy of Dr. John D. Murray: pages 10/11, 38/39.
Explanatory illustrations by Ed Stuart; activity illustrations by Richard Coombes;
headbands by Antonia Phillips.

Edited text and captions based on *An Illustrated Guide to Rocks and Minerals*
by Michael O'Donoghue.

For World Book:
Editor-in-Chief: Paul A. Kobasa
Editorial: Shawn Brennan, Lisa Kwon, Maureen Liebenson,
  Christine Sullivan
Research: Mike Barr, Madolynn Cronk, Lynn Durbin, Cheryl Graham,
  Jacqueline Jasek, Karen McCormack, and Loranne Shields
Librarian: Stephanie Kitchen
Permissions: Janet Peterson
Graphics and Design: Sandra Dyrlund, Isaiah Sheppard
Indexing: Aamir Burki, David Pofelski
Pre-press and Manufacturing: Carma Fazio, Anne Fritzinger,
  Steven Hueppchen, Madelyn Underwood
Text Processing: Curley Hunter, Gwendolyn Johnson
Proofreading: Anne Dillon

Printed in China
2 3 4 5 6 7 8 9 10 09 08 07 06

Collectors' Code

1 **Always go collecting with a friend,** and always tell an adult where you are going.

2 **Don't damage the site** and don't take more than one specimen of each rock or mineral—leave something for other collectors.

3 **Wear a hard hat** if you are exploring below a cliff. Check the cliff face carefully before you go near it, because loose rocks can sometimes fall.

4 **Ask permission before exploring** sites on private land.

5 **Leave fence gates as you find them.**

Contents

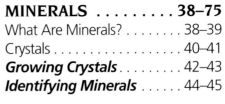

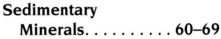

Entries ***like this*** indicate pages
featuring projects you can do!

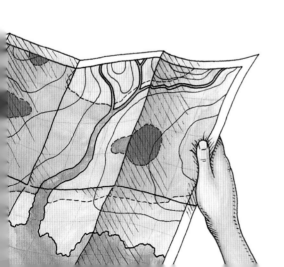

Introduction To Rocks & Minerals

Rocks are everywhere you go. You'll see them by the roadside, as pebbles on the beach, in cliffs, and exposed on mountains. They are the raw materials of bricks and concrete. Tiny fragments of rock make up a part of the soil in which plants grow.

More important, rocks shape the world we live in. If you understand rocks, you know why the landscape is the shape it is. You can understand why some soil is good for growing plants and some is not.

How this book works

This book is divided into two halves. Go to **Rocks,** which starts on page 10, to learn about the three main types of rocks and how they have made the many different landscapes of the world. You can also find out where to go and see the best examples of these landscapes.

In **Minerals,** which starts on page 38, the most common minerals and where they occur are listed. The minerals are grouped by the type of rock in which they are found. So, if you have sedimentary rocks in your area, you can see which minerals you are likely to find in them.

You can go looking for mineral specimens, but you may also get some of your mineral specimens from a rock store or museum shop. If you want to check your specimens to see what they are, you can find out how to test them on pages 44–45.

You can see which rocks and minerals belong to which group by looking at the picture band at the top of each page. These bands are also shown under the picture on this page.

The first rocks

Earth is about 4.6 billion years old. The oldest rocks that have been found were created by volcanic eruptions over the course of hundreds of millions of years. These rocks are still being made every time a volcano erupts. They are called igneous rocks, from a Latin word meaning "like fire."

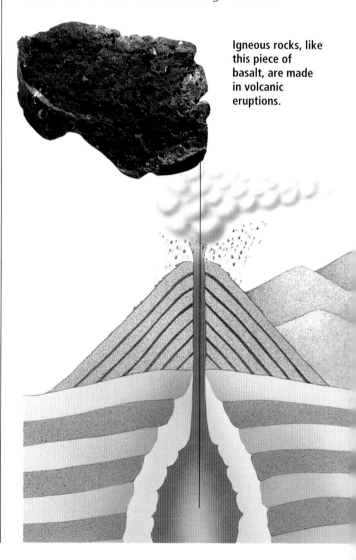

Igneous rocks, like this piece of basalt, are made in volcanic eruptions.

Igneous

Rocks from the sea

Water and wind gradually wear down igneous rocks, in a process called erosion. The rocks break up into small pieces—sediments—some of which are carried by rivers into the sea. The pieces come to rest at the bottom of the sea and form sandwichlike layers—called sedimentary layers. There is enormous pressure from the weight of the water on the seabed. Over millions of years, this pressure causes the layers of sediment to form into a type of rock called sedimentary rock.

Altered rocks

Another group of rocks is created when existing igneous and sedimentary rocks are subjected to great heat, or pressure, or both. Such rocks are called metamorphic rocks, because their mineral ingredients have been changed.

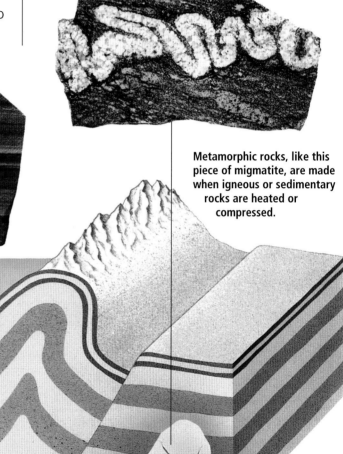

Sedimentary rocks, like this piece of sandstone, are formed under the sea by pressure.

Metamorphic rocks, like this piece of migmatite, are made when igneous or sedimentary rocks are heated or compressed.

 **Sedimentary**

 **Metamorphic**

How Rocks Move

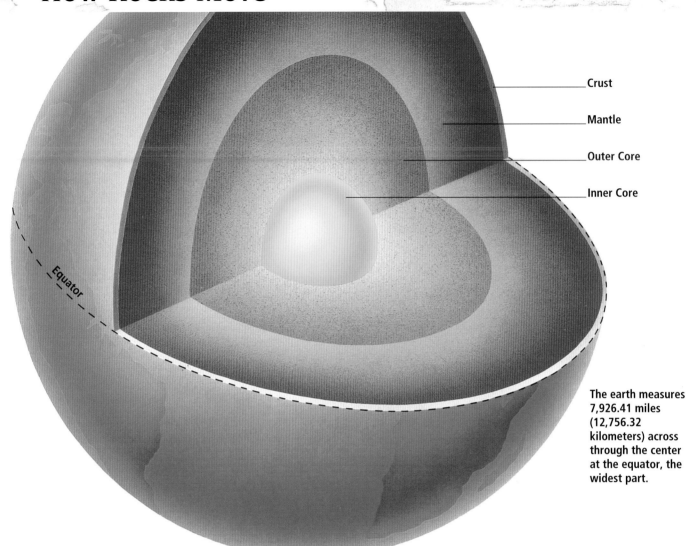

Crust

Mantle

Outer Core

Inner Core

Equator

The earth measures 7,926.41 miles (12,756.32 kilometers) across through the center at the equator, the widest part.

Did you know that fossilized fish have sometimes been found on top of mountains? To discover how this could happen, you have to learn about what goes on under the earth's crust.

The crust (the outermost layer) of the earth is very thin compared with its other layers. On a globe 1 foot (0.3 meter) across, the crust would be no thicker than a sheet of paper. In actual fact, the depth of the crust varies. It averages about 25 miles (40 kilometers) thick under the continents, but it only averages about 5 miles (8 kilometers) thick under the oceans.

Under the surface

Immediately below the crust is the mantle, which is a very thick layer of rock. The mantle is about 1,800 miles (2,900 kilometers) thick. Inside the mantle is the outer core, probably made of molten iron and nickel. It is about 1,400 miles (2,250 kilometers) thick. The inner core is probably a solid ball of iron and nickel about 1,600 miles (2,600 kilometers) across. As you go toward earth's center, the temperature gradually gets hotter. The temperature at the inner core is about 9000 °Fahrenheit (5000 °Celsius) (water's boiling point is 212 °Fahrenheit, 100 °Celsius).

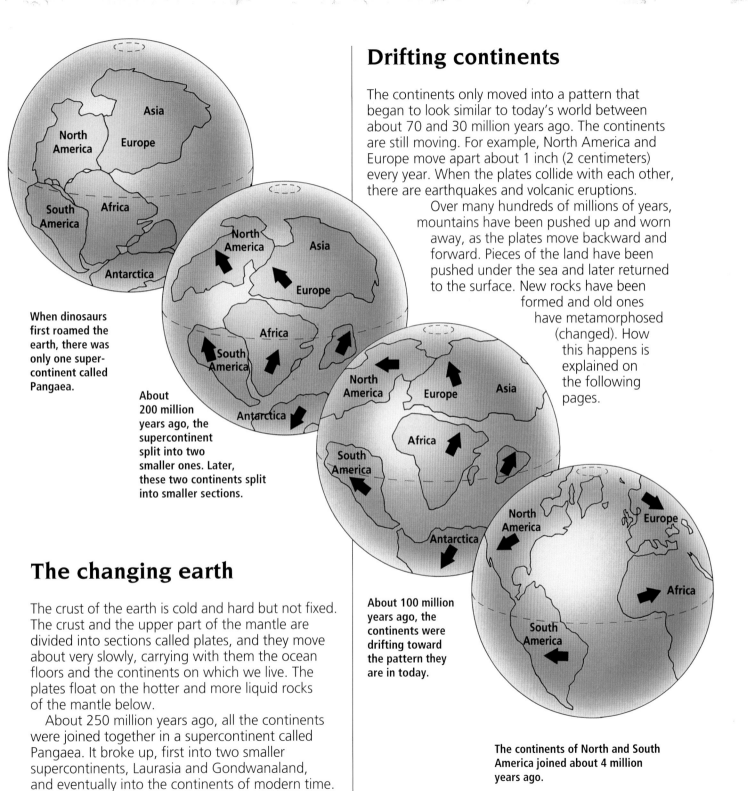

Drifting continents

The continents only moved into a pattern that began to look similar to today's world between about 70 and 30 million years ago. The continents are still moving. For example, North America and Europe move apart about 1 inch (2 centimeters) every year. When the plates collide with each other, there are earthquakes and volcanic eruptions.

Over many hundreds of millions of years, mountains have been pushed up and worn away, as the plates move backward and forward. Pieces of the land have been pushed under the sea and later returned to the surface. New rocks have been formed and old ones have metamorphosed (changed). How this happens is explained on the following pages.

When dinosaurs first roamed the earth, there was only one super-continent called Pangaea.

About 200 million years ago, the supercontinent split into two smaller ones. Later, these two continents split into smaller sections.

The changing earth

The crust of the earth is cold and hard but not fixed. The crust and the upper part of the mantle are divided into sections called plates, and they move about very slowly, carrying with them the ocean floors and the continents on which we live. The plates float on the hotter and more liquid rocks of the mantle below.

About 250 million years ago, all the continents were joined together in a supercontinent called Pangaea. It broke up, first into two smaller supercontinents, Laurasia and Gondwanaland, and eventually into the continents of modern time.

About 100 million years ago, the continents were drifting toward the pattern they are in today.

The continents of North and South America joined about 4 million years ago.

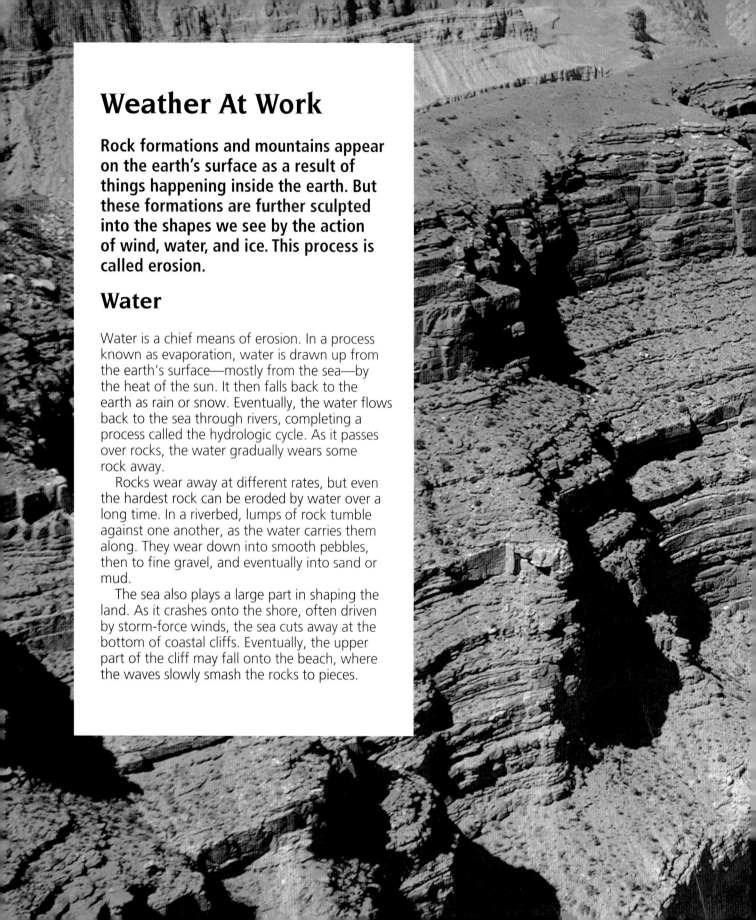

Weather At Work

Rock formations and mountains appear on the earth's surface as a result of things happening inside the earth. But these formations are further sculpted into the shapes we see by the action of wind, water, and ice. This process is called erosion.

Water

Water is a chief means of erosion. In a process known as evaporation, water is drawn up from the earth's surface—mostly from the sea—by the heat of the sun. It then falls back to the earth as rain or snow. Eventually, the water flows back to the sea through rivers, completing a process called the hydrologic cycle. As it passes over rocks, the water gradually wears some rock away.

Rocks wear away at different rates, but even the hardest rock can be eroded by water over a long time. In a riverbed, lumps of rock tumble against one another, as the water carries them along. They wear down into smooth pebbles, then to fine gravel, and eventually into sand or mud.

The sea also plays a large part in shaping the land. As it crashes onto the shore, often driven by storm-force winds, the sea cuts away at the bottom of coastal cliffs. Eventually, the upper part of the cliff may fall onto the beach, where the waves slowly smash the rocks to pieces.

Wind power

When sand and fine soil are exposed to the wind, they may be blown around. Sand dunes are formed in this way. Dunes are always changing in shape and can move great distances. Wind also drives the rain harder onto exposed rock and so helps the water to erode it more quickly. This spectacular example of wind erosion is in Utah.

How is soil made?

Soil is made from the very finest rock fragments (such as clay or sand) that are then mixed with humus. Humus is the dark brown material formed when plants and the bodies of insects and small animals decay. The humus fills the spaces between the rock particles.

Soil varies according to the sort of rock it is made from. For example, sandy soils come from sandstone, and chalky soils from limestone. Black sand comes from eroded igneous rock.

Plants need humus to survive. Humus feeds them and supplies them with water. Sand beaches have very little humus, and so few plants grow there.

Igneous Rocks

Igneous rocks start out as fiery hot, melted rock—called magma—that rises from deep beneath the earth's surface. Igneous means fiery.

When magma flows onto the earth's surface, such as when a volcano erupts, it is then called lava. The lava cools quickly and hardens to form glassy or fine-grained rocks called extrusive igneous rocks.

Igneous rocks are the main rocks under the deep-ocean beds. The earth forms new crust at underwater ocean ridges, like the Mid-Atlantic Ridge, from the lava that is released as the plates of the ocean floor spread apart.

Underground cooling

Some magma slowly cools and hardens into rock while still underground. Rocks formed this way are called intrusive igneous rocks. These slower-cooling rocks are generally coarser-grained than extrusive rocks and may include large crystals. Sometimes magma solidifies into a huge mass of igneous rock deep underground—this is called a batholith. There is an enormous batholith under the Sierra Nevada in California, and an even bigger one under the Coast Range in British Columbia, Canada. If magma finds a horizontal crack in the crust, it may form a flat sheet of volcanic rock—this is called a sill. If magma flows into a vertical crack and hardens, the result is called a dike.

A volcanic plug is more resistant than the softer rocks around it. When the softer rocks have been eroded by wind and rain, the plug is left to stand alone.

Igneous Extrusions

Andesite

Andesite is a typical rock of lava flows and volcanic environments. It is named for the Andes Mountains of South America, where major deposits of andesite are found. Andesite is also in many other locations, including all around the Pacific Ring of Fire, and in the Sierra Nevada, in California. Andesite is blackish-brown or green, with crystals of plagioclase feldspar (feldspar rich in calcium or sodium that forms at extremely hot temperatures) and materials such as biotite, hornblende, and augite.
It is used as a building material. The mineral copper is sometimes found with andesite.

Obsidian

Obsidian is a natural glass that forms when magma has cooled very quickly. It is usually gray to black, though it may have reddish or rainbow-colored streaks. Eventually, after a long period of time, it deteriorates into an ordinary looking, fine-grained rock. Locations where it is found include Mexico, Iceland, and Japan. A spectacular outcrop is at Obsidian Cliff, in Yellowstone National Park in the northwest of the United States. Obsidian is named after Obsius, a Roman who is said to have discovered the stone in Ethiopia.

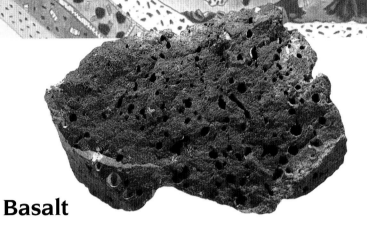

Basalt

Basalt is a hard, very fine-grained igneous rock, mostly black, very dark gray, or brown in color. It is the most common volcanic rock in the earth's crust. It flows out from volcanoes to form large sheets, called traps. Large beds of it are found in North America near the Columbia and Snake rivers. It also is found under the sea, covered by mud and other sediments. An unusual basalt formation is the Giant's Causeway in Northern Ireland. There, the basalt has formed thousands of six-sided columns. The name basalt derives from the ancient Greek word for "touchstone." This Greek word was derived from an Egyptian word for the rock.

Rhyolite

Rhyolite is formed when a very thick, sticky magma cools rapidly. It is often in volcanic domes and chimneys. Sometimes, the rapid cooling produces many curved cracks that cause the rock to break into perlite. Uses of perlite include making insulation and concrete. Round obsidian pieces found in the perlite, called Apache tears, are used in jewelry. Rhyolite is light in color. Its name comes from two Greek words meaning "stream" and "stone."

Igneous Intrusions

Intrusive igneous rocks form from magma that does not rise all the way to the earth's surface. They appear in such structures as batholiths, dikes, and sills (see page 10).

Gabbro

Several igneous rocks are called gabbro. Most of them are coarse-grained and granular in texture. Their main components are calcium-rich plagioclase feldspar and pyroxene. Gabbros tend to be darker than diorite. Olivine gabbro is a variety in which olivine forms a significant component. The color of gabbro is gray with tinges of green, brown, or violet. Few gabbros are usable as building stone, but olivine gabbro is an important source of olivine. The name comes from an Italian word meaning "smooth" or "bald."

Anorthosite

Anorthosite is white or light gray, and it has a medium- or coarse-grained texture. It is found in such areas as Norway, Newfoundland and Labrador in Canada, and the Adirondacks in the United States. It is named after anorthite—one of the plagioclase feldspars—which forms anorthosite's main component. Some anorthosite is used for ornamental building stone.

Diorite

Diorite is the name given to several similar medium- to coarse-grained rocks. These rocks consist mainly of light-colored plagioclase feldspar (feldspar rich in calcium or sodium formed in extremely hot temperatures) and smaller amounts of such dark-colored materials as biotite, hornblende, or pyroxene. Polished slabs of this grayish rock are used as building stone. The name comes from a Greek word meaning "to distinguish."

Dunite

Dunite is composed mainly of the mineral olivine. From this comes its other name, olivinite. It is a medium- to coarse-grained rock, light green in color. It is named for Mount Dun in New Zealand, where there are large deposits. It is the parent rock for some deposits of chromium and platinum.

Peridotite

Peridotite is a granular rock made up of coarse crystals. Its color ranges from light to dark green because of one of its main components, olivine. Its other main component is pyroxene. It is found worldwide, with large deposits in the Alps, the Appalachians, and mountains along the Pacific Coast of the Americas. It often occurs with deposits of metals such as nickel, chromium, and platinum.

Granite

Granite and similar rocks are among the most common rocks on the earth's continents. Granite forms huge batholiths—masses of rock—that were originally below the earth's surface (see page 10). Granite also appears as sills and veins in other rocks. The color ranges from white through light gray, pink, and pale yellow. Granite's main components are feldspars (mostly microcline and orthoclase) and quartz, along with smaller amounts of such darker-colored minerals as biotite and hornblende. The grain size is coarse. Granite is often used as a building stone. The name comes from the Latin word for "to grain" or "granulated."

Syenite

Syenite is a medium- to coarse-grained rock, ranging in color from gray through pink or pale green. It is often found in association with granite. The main components are similar to granite, but with only a tiny amount of quartz. It is often used in the form of polished slabs in building construction. The name comes from Syene in Egypt, where a similar rock containing much more quartz was first identified.

Kimberlite

Kimberlite is a form of peridotite (see above), which contains fragments of rock formed separately at an earlier time. The grain size varies. Kimberlite is one of the main types of rock in which diamonds are found. It generally occurs as pipes—cylinder-shaped channels that once carried magma (melted rock) toward the earth's surface. It is named after Kimberley, South Africa, one of the world's richest diamond areas. Its many component minerals include olivine, garnet, pyroxene, diopside, and calcite. Its color can be bluish, greenish, or black underground. But at surface level it often weathers to a yellow color.

Volcanoes

A volcano is an opening in the earth's surface through which lava (melted rock), hot gases, and rock fragments escape from the earth's interior. A volcano that can still erupt is said to be active.

A volcano that has not erupted for a long time is said to be dormant or inactive. Some volcanoes, like Aconcagua in Argentina, have not erupted for thousands of years. They are said to be extinct. The vent of an extinct or a dormant volcano may be filled with cooled lava, which has become solid rock and is called a plug.

How do volcanoes erupt?

Magma (melted rock below the earth's surface) mixes with hot gases and rises toward the earth's surface. When it finds a weak spot in the surface, it bursts through to form a volcano. Volcanoes release several kinds of material: lava, rock fragments, ash, dust, and gas. Lava is the name given to the magma when it flows out onto the earth's surface. The lava is a glowing, sticky mass that hardens into igneous rock when it comes into contact with air or water.

Where are the volcanoes?

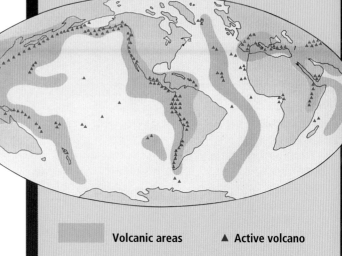

Volcanic areas	▲ Active volcano

Most volcanoes are found near the edges of the continental plates that cover the earth (see page 7). Mount St. Helens in Washington, for example, which was inactive from 1857 to 1980 (when it erupted violently), is close to the junction between the Pacific and the North American plates. The ring of volcanoes all round the Pacific Ocean is sometimes called the Ring of Fire. There are also many volcanoes under the sea, particularly along the midocean ridges.

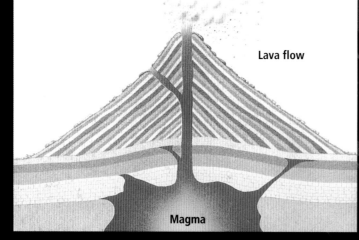

Lava flow

Magma

Sedimentary Rocks

The earth is continually recycling its crust. Even as some mountains are being formed, others are being steadily worn away, and the fragments are washed down into lakes, rivers, and the sea. These fragments are called sediments. They settle to the bottom of bodies of water, building up layer upon layer of mud and sand. Over thousands of years, under the pressure of the upper layers, these accumulated layers form new rocks, called sedimentary rocks.

The raw materials

The type of sediments from which these new rocks are formed depends on the minerals that were in the original fragments. Some sediments are pieces of older rocks that have been worn away by the weather. They include sand, which is made up mainly of quartz, and clay.

Rocks made chiefly of sand are called sandstones. They were built up in lakes and estuaries, but some were originally loose sand deposited into dunes by the wind. Other sedimentary rocks are formed as a result of chemical action. Calcium carbonates that crystallize out of water form limestones. Chalk is one form of limestone. Chalk beds also contain the chalky skeletons of millions of tiny sea animals.

Sediments form successive layers called beds. When these layers become rock, geologists call them strata, which means layers. The loose material of the sediments are cemented together by minerals and pressure. Most of the pressure comes from the weight of more and more layers building up over long periods of time. Upheavals in the crust can also add pressure. These forces, acting on sediments, create sedimentary rocks.

The finest example of sedimentary beds can be seen in the Grand Canyon in Arizona. There, layers of different rocks up to 1 mile (1.5 kilometers) deep are exposed. The Grand Canyon has been cut by the waters of the Colorado River, but the land has also been rising over time.

Sedimentary Rocks

Breccia

This is a mixture of angular rock fragments held together in a fine-grained natural cement. The fragments may be from many different types of rocks. The angular shapes show that the rock pieces were exposed to little weathering before becoming part of the sediment layer. Breccia is often found as a result of the folding and fracturing of rocks. It is an ornamental building stone.

Conglomerate

This is made of lumps and pebbles of rock, sometimes of several kinds, in a fine-grained natural cement. The pebbles are rounded, showing that they were worn smooth by water or wind before being buried by layers of sediment. When a pebbly beach is buried and eventually turns into rock, the result is conglomerate. It can be used for building. A variety of conglomerate with a colorful contrast between the gravel and the cement binding it is called pudding stone.

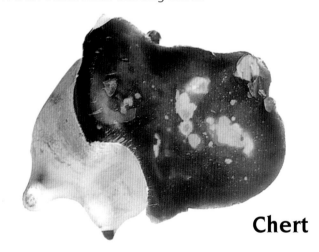

Chert

This occurs as nodules, when it is called flint, or as veins in other rocks. It is a mixture of silica with traces of calcite and other minerals. Chert formed from the silica in the remains of diatoms and of the skeletons and shells of tiny sea organisms called radiolaria, is called radiolarite. Varieties of chert also include agate, chrysoprase, and onyx.

Dolomite

A soft rock found in many parts of the world, including the Dolomite Mountains of Italy and many other mountain ranges. Dolomite is formed out of limestone, coral, or marble by the chemical changes caused by dissolved magnesium. Light gray or yellow in color, it is used for building.

Graywacke

This rock—a hard, grayish sandstone—is made from rock fragments and silt sediments that are deposited in deep water. Graywacke is dark gray, brown, or green in color. It contains grains of quartz, feldspar, and fragments of other rocks in a clayish matrix (rock in which other minerals are embedded). It is found worldwide, usually in thick bands.

Sandstone

This is the name of a group of sedimentary rocks made up of sand-sized grains. Most of the grains are quartz and vary in size from 0.07 inches (2 millimeters) to 0.002 inches (0.063 millimeters). Sandstone's color varies from cream through gray, yellow, green, and red to brown. The cement binding the grains is usually quartz. One of the commonest sedimentary rocks, sandstone is used as a building material; the brownstone buildings of New York City are built of sandstone.

Clay

This name describes a very fine-grained sediment, as well as several types of rock that form from it. Clay is soft and pliable when wet. When baked, it becomes hard and is used to make roof tiles, dishes, flower pots, and many other household items.

Shale is a fine-grained clay rock formed when mud is compressed. It can easily be broken into layers. Another clay rock, known as mudstone, is similar to shale but does not break into definite layers. Siltstones and marl are also varieties of mudstone.

Limestone Caves

All rain is slightly acidic. Some of the acid in rain water comes from natural sources, such as carbon dioxide that is absorbed from the air, or the gases emitted during a volcanic eruption. Other acids come from pollution. Sulfur dioxides and nitrogen oxides that are released into the air by cars, factories, and power plants also cause water to become more acidic. We call this polluted water acid rain.

Whatever its source, the acid in water will dissolve certain rocks over time, particularly limestone. In addition to being vulnerable to acidic water, the naturally occurring vertical and horizontal faults (cracks) in limestone allow water to pool and collect. Over time, the pooled water dissolves the stone and causes the size of the fault to increase.

This process can lead to amazing limestone formations. Water flowing through such stone may eventually form underground rivers, and these rivers can in turn carve out huge caves. The Mammoth-Flint Ridge Cave System in the United States is an example. This cave system features more than 300 miles (480 kilometers) of caverns, passages, lakes, and rivers.

Stalactites and stalagmites

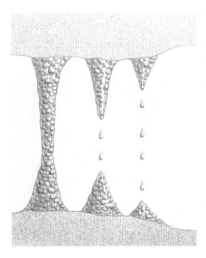

Water dissolves limestone as it seeps through it. As this limestone-laden water drips from the roof of a cave, it will (over hundreds of years) form a stalactite. Below the drip, a stalagmite will rise from the floor. Sometimes they join up to make a pillar.

Limestone

This rock is made up mostly of calcite, a mineral form of calcium carbonate. Most seawater and fresh water contains dissolved calcium carbonate. When water evaporates, the calcium carbonate left behind may settle on the muddy sea floor. The calcium-rich mud may eventually form limestone.

Limestone cave system

1 Limestone cliff with a network of cracks
2 Cave with a spring where stalactites and stalagmites are forming
3 Cave formed when the ceiling collapsed
4 Rubble from the collapsed ceiling
5 Underground stream flowing from the spring
6 Cave with a lake. At one time the river would have flowed out of the cave entrance (7)
8 Underground river flowing out of the lake and reaching the open air as a waterfall down the side of the cliff

Find Out About Limestone

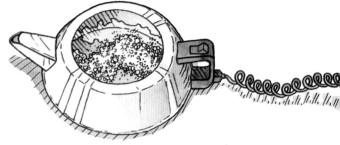

Stalactites can grow anywhere that water is hard, even in your own home. The hardness or softness of your water depends on what kinds of rock and soil the water has flowed through after it fell as rain.

Testing for hard water

The hardness of water comes from having more of certain minerals, mainly ones containing calcium and magnesium, dissolved in the water. When water is heated or evaporates, it leaves behind calcium and magnesium carbonates. Calcite (the mineral form of calcium carbonate) is what stalactites and stalagmites are made from (see page 20).

You can easily find out if your water is hard or soft by seeing how well soap lathers in it. If it lathers well, then the water is soft. If it doesn't, the water is hard.

Over time, hard water can leave deposits, called scale, on items with which it comes in contact, such as pipes or cooking utensils. You can buy a chemical to descale items, such as electric coffeemakers or shower heads. These chemicals begin to fizz as they dissolve the lime scale away. **Be careful not to breathe the fumes from the descaler—they will harm your lungs!**

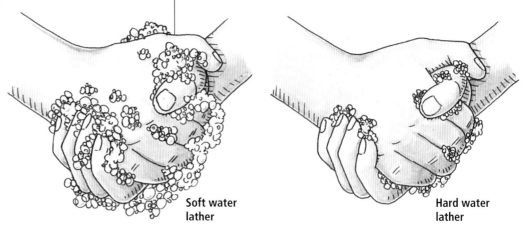

Soft water lather

Hard water lather

Looking for stalactites

The best place to see stalactites is, of course, in a limestone cave. But stalactites can form in other, unexpected places.

For instance, stalactites sometimes form under old bridges or short tunnels where the ground above is very damp. The chances are that the water will drip through the bridge, especially if it is built of brick. If it does, tiny stalactites will sometimes form on the underside of the bridge or tunnel, just as they would in a cave.

It's easy to remember the difference between the two kinds of formations! Stalac**tite**s hold **tight** to the ceiling, while stalag**mite**s **might** one day reach it.

Grow a stalactite

You can grow your own stalactites and stalagmites at home by following these instructions:

1 **Collect the following items:** a large mixing bowl, 2 large glass jelly jars, an old saucer, some yarn, and a large packet of borax. (You can buy borax [washing soda] from a supermarket or grocery store.)

2 **Ask an adult to help** you heat enough water to fill the two jars. The adult should pour the hot water into the mixing bowl, then slowly add the borax, stirring continually until the borax crystals are mostly dissolved.

3 **Pour the mixture into the jars** and place them about 10 inches (25 centimeters) apart on a flat surface. Put the saucer between them.

4 **Make a rope** by twisting or braiding 10 or 12 pieces of yarn together. The rope should be about 2 feet (0.6 meter) long. Sink one of the rope ends into each jar, so that it forms a gentle curve between the jars with the lowest point over the saucer.

5 **Leave the jars and rope** set up for 4 to 5 days. If there are smaller children or pets in your home, this experiment must be set up well out of their reach. **Borax is poisonous.** The solution of water and borax is absorbed up the rope from each jar. You will find that little stalactites form in the center as the water dries from the rope. Some of the water will drip into the saucer and a tiny stalagmite will start to grow underneath.

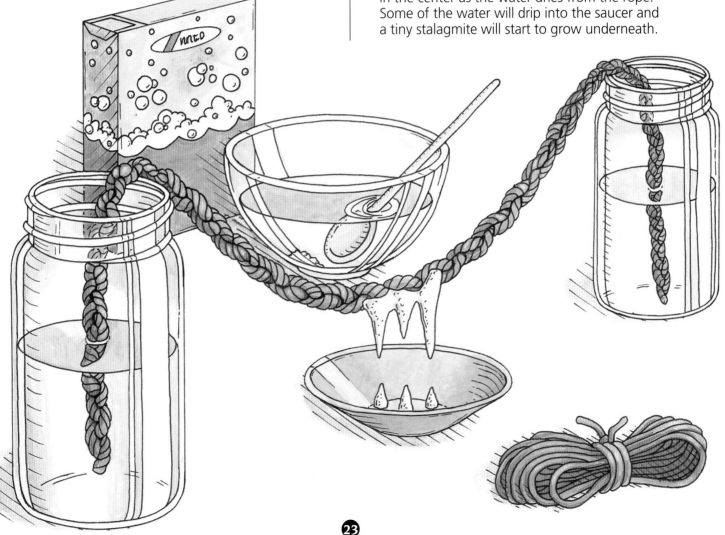

Rocks In Rivers

Much sandstone results from material deposited in rivers. Moving water carries the tiny rock fragments suspended in it. As the river makes a turn, the fragments settle on the inside of the curve where the water moves more slowly. Rivers also slow down and drop materials as they flow into a lake or an ocean.

A riverbed may contain many different kinds of rocks, particularly in a mountainous region. Most of the boulders will have been there from before the time when the river started flowing. The boulders will look rounded because they have been eroded by the river. Other rocks will have been carried down from upstream.

In places where the river slows down, it drops the heavier particles. Minerals that collect in such spots are called placer deposits. The name comes from a Spanish word meaning "sandbank." People have found valuable minerals such as diamonds, gold, platinum, and tin in placer deposits.

Because the minerals are heavier than the rest of the sand and gravel in the riverbed, they can be separated by panning—washing them in a shallow pan. The lighter material rinses away, leaving the heavier minerals behind.

Placer formation

A river picks up sediments and rocks, as it flows toward the sea.

As the river goes round a curve, it drops sediments on the inner side of the curve, forming a placer.

Sometimes, as more and more sediment is deposited, the bend of the river is cut off and forms a small lobe; the river begins to follow a straight course again. (See the middle and bottom pictures at left.)

The Seashore

The seashore is a good place to look for rocks. But it can also be very dangerous if the beach is so narrow that you cannot escape from an incoming tide, or if there are cliffs from which rocks may fall. Geologists always wear hardhats when they work near the foot of a cliff.

The face of a sea cliff is well worth studying. The strata (layers) of sedimentary rocks can often be seen there, perhaps cut by dikes of igneous rock such as granite. Fold patterns, which show how rocks have been distorted and folded over millions of years, may also be observed.

The rocks, pebbles, and sand on the beach are graded (sorted) by the waves. They range in size from quite large pebbles down to very small ones, and finally to sand, which is mostly quartz.

Amber is sometimes washed up on beaches. This gem material is fossilized resin from prehistoric pine trees. It is common on Central American beaches, but the best amber comes from the shores of the Baltic Sea. (Most amber does not appear on seashores, but is mined from claylike soil known as blue earth.) Sometimes a lump of amber will contain a fly, leaf, or seed that was trapped and preserved by the flowing resin hundreds of thousands of years ago.

Pebble beaches

The kinds of pebbles on a beach depend on the rocks nearby. A high coastal cliff may contain several kinds of rock. As pieces of rock fall down to the beach and are tumbled by the waves, they turn into pebbles.

Igneous rocks are more likely to turn into pebbles than many sedimentary rocks, because they are much harder and do not wear away so readily. For example, in granite country, you will find pink or gray mottled pebbles, while basalt country produces black pebbles.

In chalk regions many of the pebbles will be of flint. They may not be obvious, because they develop a soft, light-colored coating, which hides the hard, dark gray rock inside. Sometimes there are heavy stones with shiny metallic yellow sparkles. Some people have mistaken these rocks for gold, but they are pyrite—also known as "fool's gold."

A few pebbles appear to be green or brown gemstones, but they are usually colored glass, called sea glass, made from old bottles that have been broken up and smoothed into pebbles. Bricks and lumps of concrete may also be broken up and worn down into pebbles.

Metamorphic Rocks

Metamorphic rocks are those that have been changed inside the earth's crust by great heat and pressure, or chemical activity. Both igneous and sedimentary rocks can be metamorphosed, a word that means "changed completely."

Some rocks are metamorphosed over thousands of square miles in a process called regional metamorphism. Heat from below the deepest level of solid rock, enormous pressure from layers of overlaying rock, and pressure from movement in the earth's crust, such as earthquakes, can act together or separately to change rock.

Contact metamorphism occurs when heat from nearby magma (melted rock) causes recrystallization, or the formation of new minerals, in the "parent" rock. Contact metamorphism usually is found in rock that is next to an intrusion—a spot where magma thrusts up toward the surface through the parent rock.

Many metamorphic rocks, like gneisses, can be easily identified by their striped or banded appearance. Gneisses are formed under considerable pressure.

Metamorphic Rocks

Hornfels

Hornfels is a contact metamorphic rock derived from clays. The main minerals in hornfels may include quartz, feldspars, andalusite, and biotite, depending on the composition of the original rock from which the hornfels was formed. The color of the rock is usually a dark gray, blue, green, or black. Hornfels occurs in many locations, including the Sierra Nevada in California. Its name comes from a German word meaning "horn rock," referring to its luster.

Marble

Marble is formed by both regional and contact metamorphism. The parent rock is limestone, recrystallized, and the main mineral is calcite or dolomite. The colors of marble vary from pure white to a mosaic of red, green, or brown streaks and patches. Marble is found all over the world, sometimes in huge quantities. One of the most famous types of marble comes from Carrara in Italy. It has been used by sculptors for hundreds of years. The name marble comes from a Greek word meaning "gleaming stone."

Skarn

Skarn is formed by the metamorphosis of limestones or dolomites in contact with silica-rich rock, usually granite. Heat and pressure cause the silica-rich rock to release volatile fluids containing one or more of the elements aluminum, iron, and magnesium. As the fluid seeps into the limestone or dolomite, the elements replace some of the calcite in these rocks. Skarn is common in the United States and many other countries. Deposits of minerals such as copper, iron, and zinc often run through skarn.

Slate

Slate is a contact metamorphic rock; the parent sedimentary rock is most often clay or shale. The main minerals in slate include biotite, chlorite, muscovite, and quartz. It is found worldwide, especially in France, Scotland, Wales, southern Germany, and the northeastern United States. Slate is usually gray or black. It splits easily into thin sheets, which are used for roofing and as flagstones. The name comes from an Old French word meaning "split piece."

Gneiss

Gneiss (pronounced "nice") is a regional metamorphosed rock. Gneiss formed from sedimentary rock is called paragneiss. Orthogneiss is formed from igneous rock. The main minerals in gneiss include light-colored feldspars, quartz, and dark-colored minerals such as biotite, muscovite, or hornblende. Gneiss is coarse-grained, with irregular banding. The color varies from light, in gneisses derived from granite, to dark, in rocks derived from sandstones. Gneiss occurs worldwide. There are large deposits in eastern Canada, the northeastern United States, Greenland, northern Europe, and Russia. It is sometimes used as a building stone. The name comes from an old German word meaning "sparks" because of small bits of minerals like quartz or biotite and muscovite mica that sparkle in the rock.

Quartzite

Quartzite is a very hard regional metamorphic rock made up mostly or entirely of the mineral quartz, from which it gets its name. The parent rocks are many kinds of quartz-rich sedimentary rocks—for example, sandstone. Pure quartzite is white, but if other minerals are present it may be gray, brown, green, or red. Quartzite is found worldwide. Places where it is found in the United States include the Carolinas. There are large deposits in Spain, India, and China. Quartzite is used for floors, facing stone in building, and in glass and ceramics.

Schist

Schist is the name given to a variety of regional metamorphic rocks, which vary according to the main minerals in them, their parent rocks, and the amount of heat and pressure under which they were formed. Schists can be identified by the parallel arrangement of most of their minerals, which causes them to split easily into layered slabs. The name schist comes from a Greek word meaning "to split."

Mica schists come from clayish sedimentary rocks and contain mica (biotite and muscovite) and quartz. The main mineral in chlorite schists is chorite. Talc schist is greasy to the touch, like the mineral talc, which is its main ingredient.

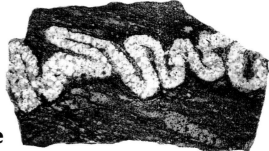

Migmatite

Migmatite is the name given to a composite rock which is a mixture of two types of rocks. The country (original) rock is some kind of sedimentary or igneous rock that is changed to metamorphic rock when magma (melted rock) gets injected into it. When the magma hardens, it forms streaks and veins mixed through the parent rock. The formation of migmatite takes place far below the earth's surface. The name comes from a Greek word meaning "mixture." Migmatite is used as building stone.

Plants Turn Into Rocks

Coal is a soft rock, colored black or brown. Unlike most other rocks, coal was formed from organic (living) material. It is the fossil remains of prehistoric plants, which is why coal is called a fossil fuel.

If coal deposits are close to the surface, strip mining is used to dig them out. Powerful diggers strip away the soil and rock above the coal and heap it to one side. The coal is then dug away. Finally, the land is restored as nearly as possible to its original condition.

Most coal seams lie deep underground. To reach them, miners must sink (dig) a shaft. Then tunnels are dug along the line of the seam. The miners are taken down to their work by elevator and the coal and spoil (waste rock) are brought up in the elevator.

Coal is usually graded according to how much carbon it contains. Lignite, or brown coal, contains the least carbon. Subbituminous and bituminous coal both contain more carbon than does lignite. Bituminous coal is the most common kind and gives off the most heat. The coal containing the most carbon is anthracite, which burns slowly with almost no smoke. The countries that produce the most coal are China, the United States, India, Russia, Germany, Australia, and South Africa.

This is anthracite coal, the blackest, hardest, and oldest of all.

Trees into coal

Lignite coal

Bituminous coal

Anthracite coal

Between 360 and 286 million years ago, in the Carboniferous Period, there were huge forests of giant ferns growing in swampland.

When the ferns died, they fell into the swampy ground, where they decayed and formed a thick layer of partly rotted vegetation.

Over millions of years, as the continents moved and the climate altered, this rotting layer was covered with mud and sand.

This happened over and over again. The huge "sandwich" grew to be thousands of yards thick.

Over time, as the deeply buried layers of decayed vegetation were compressed and heated up, they were changed into seams of coal.

City Survey

You don't have to go long distances to find and study rocks. There are lots of different rocks in your own neighborhood.

Start at home

Your own house, if it is old, may be built from stone, but it is more likely to be built of clay brick. If it is a wood-frame house, it may have stone or brick in the foundation. The roof may be clay tiles.

When you look through a window, you are looking through rock. The glass in the window is made from silica sand, soda ash, and limestone.

Some older buildings are coated with stucco—a mixture of sand, water, and a cementing mixture which may contain lime. If you find such a building, you can add the mineral gypsum (see page 53) to your list.

On Main Street

The sidewalks on your street may contain rocks. If the sidewalks are not made of concrete, they are probably made of granite slabs.

You may also notice many different rocks in the buildings in the downtown area where you live. Many old buildings are made of sandstone or limestone blocks. Newer ones are more often faced with slabs of those rocks.

If you go inside a bank or office, the floor may well be of marble or some other hard, decorative stone. The steps of buildings are often stone.

Hidden rocks

Some rocks are hidden because they are made into other materials. There's the clay in bricks, for example. And, the crushed granite or basalt in the road surface can't be seen, but it is there.

Cement is a mixture of lime, silica, and alumina. The lime usually comes from limestone and the other materials from other crushed rocks. It is mixed with sand and lime to make mortar, which is used to hold bricks together. It is also mixed with crushed rock or small pebbles (called aggregate) to form concrete.

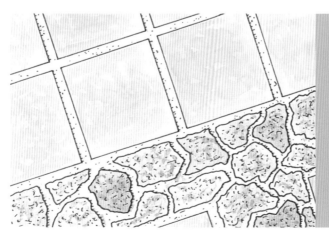

What about the yard?

Take a look in your yard or in the local park. If you have a patio, look to see what sort of slabs were used for the paving. They may be concrete, so you can put down cement and aggregate on your list. If they are stone, try to identify it. It will most likely be a sandstone. If there's a rock garden, take a close look at the rocks used to build it, and try to identify them.

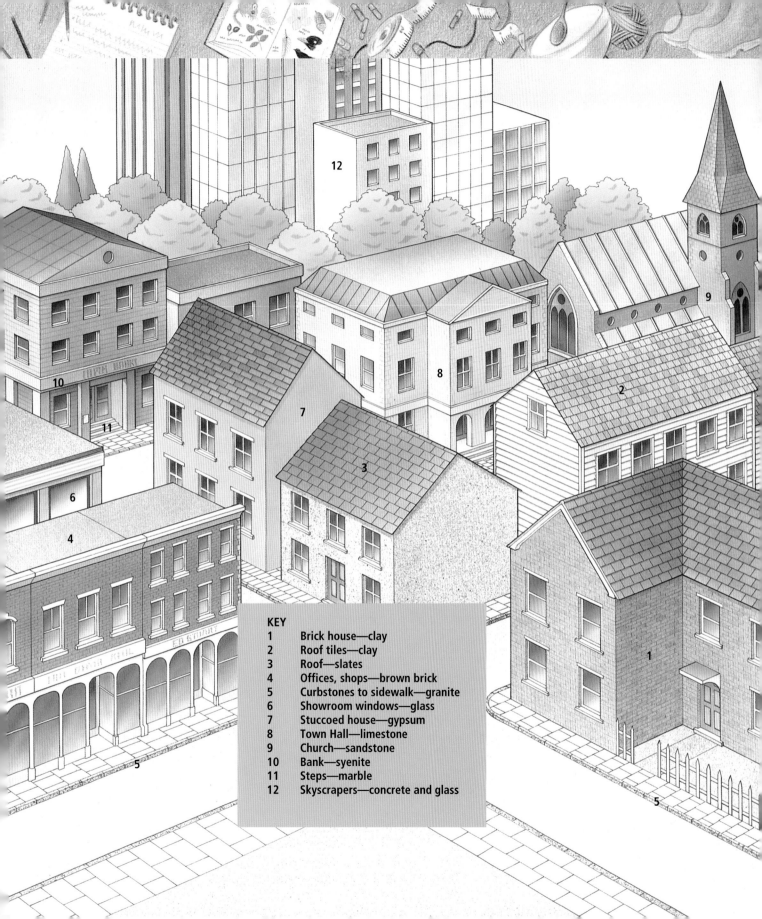

KEY
1 Brick house—clay
2 Roof tiles—clay
3 Roof—slates
4 Offices, shops—brown brick
5 Curbstones to sidewalk—granite
6 Showroom windows—glass
7 Stuccoed house—gypsum
8 Town Hall—limestone
9 Church—sandstone
10 Bank—syenite
11 Steps—marble
12 Skyscrapers—concrete and glass

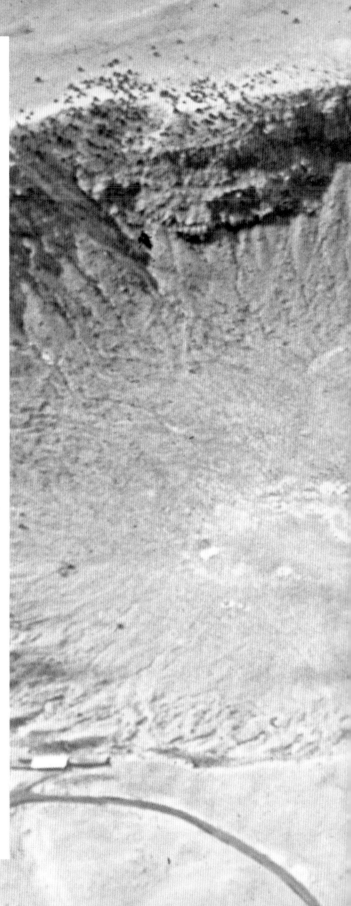

Rocks From The Sky

Meteoroids are pieces of stone or metal from outer space that enter the earth's atmosphere. Air friction makes them grow hot and glow, causing the phenomenon called shooting stars.

Most meteoroids burn up, but about 35,000 tons (32,000 metric tons) of space rubble survives to reach the earth's surface every year. Nearly all of it is space dust, or dust-sized bits of burned-up meteoroids. But a few larger pieces make it to Earth. These are called meteorites.

Giant meteorites

A number of giant meteorites have struck the earth during its 4.6-billion-year history. Most of the craters they caused have vanished, because the earth's surface has changed a great deal during that time. But you can see huge numbers of meteorite craters on the moon, and on some of the planets, because there has been no erosion to destroy the marks of the impact on their surfaces.

Some craters do remain on the earth's surface, like Meteor Crater in Arizona (shown here), which is about 50,000 years old. It measures about 4,180 feet (1,275 meters) across and was made by a meteorite measuring some 33 yards (30 meters) wide. There is another huge crater in Siberia.

Larger objects from space have hit the earth in the past. The element iridium is far more common in meteorites than in the rocks of the earth's crust. But in many places around the world, scientists have found far more iridium than usual in the layer of clay that separates the Cretaceous and Tertiary periods in the earth's strata. This is thought to have come from a small asteroid (minor planet) which hit the earth about 65 million years ago. The asteroid's crater is believed to lie in the Gulf of Mexico, and its impact may have created a cloud of dust which helped lead to the extinction of the dinosaurs.

Iron meteorite

Where do they come from?

All meteorites come from within the solar system—the planets, minor planets, and fragments that circle the sun. There are three kinds. Stony meteorites consist of minerals rich in silicon and oxygen, and they contain particles of iron. Iron meteorites are mostly iron and nickel. Stony-iron meteorites contain nearly equal amounts of silicon-based stone and iron-nickel metal.

Meteoritic iron was the first kind that people used to work into tools, ornaments, and weapons. This started about 6,000 years ago, but the use of iron did not become widespread until about 3,500 years ago.

Stony meteorite

What Are Minerals?

Just as rocks are the building blocks of the earth's crust, so minerals are the building blocks of rocks. Minerals are natural substances—not man-made. They are solid—not liquid or a gas. Each mineral has the same chemical makeup, no matter where it is found.

Minerals are made from the chemical elements. There are more than 100 elements. Ninety-three of them are known to occur naturally on or in the earth. Each element contains atoms of just one unique type. Atoms are so small that over 25 trillion of them would fit on the period at the end of this sentence.

Most minerals form in the magma (molten rock) far below the earth's surface. As the magma is pushed up toward the crust, it cools, and then some of the elements begin to crystallize—that is, combine to form little solid blocks called crystals. Minerals crystallize at different temperatures and pressures within the magma. As a result, two or more minerals can contain the same element, but put together in a different way. The minerals listed in this book are categorized under the type of rock in which they are most likely to be found.

Identifying minerals

There are several clues to identifying a mineral. They include its luster (surface shine), cleavage (splitting into flat-surfaced pieces), hardness, color, and streak. A chemist can also identify the chemical elements in each mineral. You can find out how to carry out some of these tests on pages 44–45. Each mineral shown in this book has a short data caption that tells you the identification details of that mineral. This will help you to check your specimens.

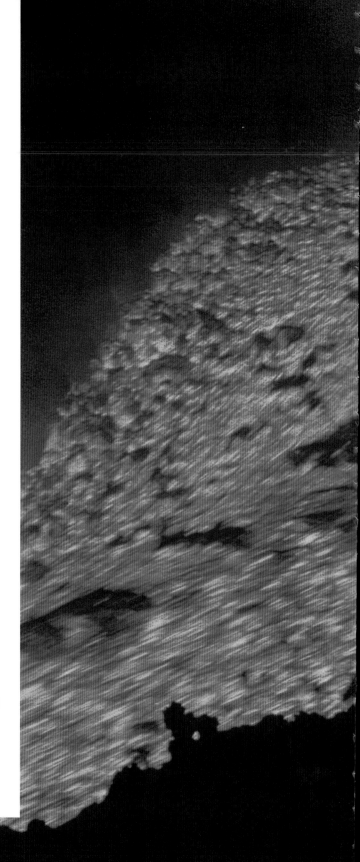

Decoding mineral recipes

The table below lists all the natural chemical elements and the abbreviations scientists use to refer to them. These abbreviations are a sort of chemical shorthand to avoid writing out long descriptions.

Most of the minerals listed in the following pages are made up of different elements. Each one has its chemical formula listed in the caption. This describes the mineral's special "recipe."

You can work out what elements are involved in each mineral by checking the abbreviations—

For example (formula for zircon—see page 48)

$$ZrSiO_4$$

1 part zirconium   1 part silicon   4 parts oxygen

Ac	Actinium	F	Fluorine	Nb	Niobium	Se	Selenium
Ag	Silver	Fe	Iron	Nd	Neodymium	Si	Silicon
Al	Aluminum	Fr	Francium	Ne	Neon	Sm	Samarium
Ar	Argon	Ga	Gallium	Ni	Nickel	Sn	Tin
As	Arsenic	Gd	Gadolinium	Np	Neptunium	Sr	Strontium
At	Astatine	Ge	Germanium	O	Oxygen	Ta	Tantalum
Au	Gold	H	Hydrogen	Os	Osmium	Tb	Terbium
B	Boron	He	Helium	P	Phosphorus	Tc	Technetium
Ba	Barium	Hf	Hafnium	Pa	Protactinium	Te	Tellurium
Be	Beryllium	Hg	Mercury	Pb	Lead	Th	Thorium
Bi	Bismuth	Ho	Holmium	Pd	Palladium	Ti	Titanium
Br	Bromine	I	Iodine	Po	Polonium	Tl	Thallium
C	Carbon	In	Indium	Pr	Praseodymium	Tm	Thulium
Ca	Calcium	Ir	Iridium	Pt	Platinum	U	Uranium
Cd	Cadmium	K	Potassium	Pu	Plutonium	V	Vanadium
Ce	Cerium	Kr	Krypton	Ra	Radium	W	Tungsten
Cl	Chlorine	La	Lanthanum	Rb	Rubidium	Xe	Xenon
Co	Cobalt	Li	Lithium	Re	Rhenium	Y	Yttrium
Cr	Chromium	Lu	Lutetium	Rh	Rhodium	Yb	Ytterbium
Cs	Cesium	Mg	Magnesium	Rn	Radon	Zn	Zinc
Cu	Copper	Mn	Manganese	Ru	Ruthenium	Zr	Zirconium
Dy	Dysprosium	Mo	Molybdenum	S	Sulfur		
Er	Erbium	N	Nitrogen	Sb	Antimony		
Eu	Europium	Na	Sodium	Sc	Scandium		

Crystals

Mineral crystals have a shape with flat surfaces and a regular pattern of atoms (see page 38), instead of being irregular lumps. Almost all minerals form crystals in the right conditions: opal is an exception.

Many crystals are formed from the cooling process that magma undergoes after it has been thrust up nearer to the surface of the earth. Some crystals, such as salt, are formed from solutions (substances dissolved in a liquid). Yet others form from the gases escaping from volcanoes—sulfur crystals are formed in this way.

Most gemstones used in jewelry have been cut from crystals. The complicated pattern of cuts, known as facets, are designed to show off the stone's color and sparkle to its best advantage.

Some crystals grow to enormous sizes. The huge gypsum crystals shown in the main picture are from the Cave of Swords at Naica in Mexico.

Crystal Shapes

The best way to learn about crystal shapes is to look at as many examples as you can—for example, in museums and rock stores. Crystal shapes are often simple but very difficult to describe in words.

Crystals can be grouped into seven basic types or systems, although there are many variations within this basic classification. Examples of crystals from the seven systems are shown on the opposite page as diagrams. In the descriptions of minerals in the following pages, the crystal system to which each mineral belongs is listed in the caption.

The seven crystal systems

Isometric system

Tetragonal system

Orthorhombic system

Monoclinic system

Triclinic system

Rhombohedral system

Hexagonal system

Growing Crystals

You can grow crystals at home by following these instructions. The crystals you make will behave the way they do in nature and will seem to grow. What they are actually doing is re-forming themselves (or crystallizing) out of a liquid. All crystals are solids, but to make crystals you must start with a liquid.

Frosted windows

If it is very cold outside, but warm inside the house, you might find beautiful frost patterns all over the cold glass. When it is below freezing outside, the warm, moist air on the inside condenses on the cold glass and forms frost crystals. The same thing happens inside cars when it is very cold. You can make this happen any time and without getting the window cold!

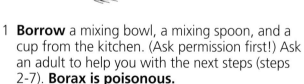

1 **Borrow** a mixing bowl, a mixing spoon, and a cup from the kitchen. (Ask permission first!) Ask an adult to help you with the next steps (steps 2-7). **Borax is poisonous.**
2 **Fill the cup with borax crystals** (washing soda) and pour them into the bowl.
3 **Fill the cup with hot water** from the tap and add it to the crystals in the bowl.

4 **Stir gently** until most of the crystals disappear.
5 **Dip a sponge or cloth into the liquid** and wipe it gently over a window. It does not matter which way you wipe, but try not to go over the same patch twice.

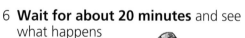

6 **Wait for about 20 minutes** and see what happens to the window.
7 **If you add some blue food dye to** the liquid, it will make the "frost" crystals look even colder. Try other colors as well (but not all at once) to see how the "frost" changes.
8 **You can do this experiment with other chemicals.** Try Epsom salts (buy them from a drugstore) or bath salts. Does the "frost" have a different pattern with a different substance?

Crystal sculptures

Crystals will form themselves around any shape offered to them. You can make use of this behavior to make crystal sculptures.

1 **Buy a pack of pipe cleaners** and ask an adult to cut them in half with wire cutters.

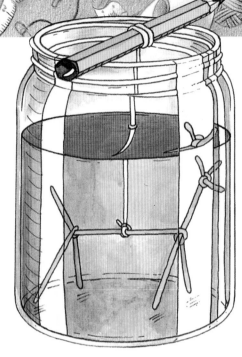

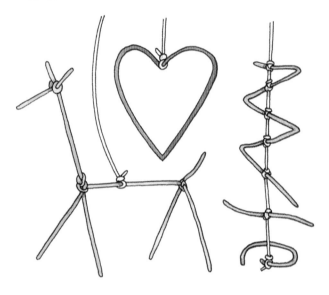

2 **Twist the pipe cleaner pieces together** to make an animal, a tree, or some other shape (see the picture for some ideas). Tie a thread to the top of the sculpture.
3 **Borrow** a mixing bowl and mixing spoon from the kitchen. (Ask permission first!)
4 **Measure out ½ cup (120 milliliters) of hot water** from the tap, and pour it into the bowl.
5 **Measure out 1 cup (240 milliliters) of Epsom salts** and pour them into the water. (You can buy Epsom salts from a supermarket or a drugstore.)
6 **Stir the mixture gently** until the Epsom salts are dissolved; then add four or five drops of food dye to the mixture. Pour the solution into a wide-mouthed glass jar and leave it to cool.

7 **Put the jar on a sunny window sill** or in another warm place. Tie the other end of the thread on the sculpture to a pencil and balance this across the mouth of the jar, so that the sculpture hangs in the solution. If pets or smaller children live in your home, **place this mixture well out of their reach**.
8 **Leave in the warm place for 2 to 3 days** while the crystals form. When you take the sculpture out, treat it very gently so that the crystals do not break off.

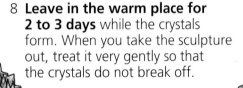

Identifying Minerals

You can identify some minerals just by looking at them. But many minerals cannot be identified with certainty by sight alone. There are simple tests you can do to find out what mineral you have.

1 You can test the mineral for its **hardness**.
2 You can test its **streak color**.
3 You can also measure its **specific gravity**.

Each mineral shown in this book has a caption that tells you which crystal system (or family) it belongs to, its streak color, its specific gravity, and a bar scale showing its hardness.

The crystal families, or crystal systems, are shown on page 41 in diagram form. Look at these two pages to see how to carry out tests for hardness, streak, and specific gravity.

1 Testing the hardness

In 1822 Friedrich Mohs, a German chemist, worked out a set of 10 sample minerals for hardness testing. Each mineral can be scratched by any mineral with the next higher number on the list. For example, diamond (10) scratches all minerals of a lower number on the hardness scale. Quartz (7) scratches feldspar (6).

Experts use special hardness testers with a splinter of each mineral set in metal holders.

Mineral	No.	Scratched by
Talc	1	fingernail (easy)
Gypsum	2	fingernail
Calcite	3	Copper coin
Fluorite	4	Penknife blade (easy)
Apatite	5	Penknife blade
Feldspar	6	Steel file (easy)
Quartz	7	Steel file
Topaz	8	Steel file (difficult)
Corundum	9	Steel file (very difficult)
Diamond	10	Scratches every other mineral substance

2 Testing the streak

The streak test gives the true color of a mineral when it is reduced to powder, which may be quite different from the color of the crystal. You can do this test by using the back (the unglazed side) of an ordinary ceramic tile. Experts use a special, rough, porcelain plate.

   When you scrape the mineral across the back of the tile, it will leave a streak of fine powder behind. You may be surprised at the difference in color. For example, pyrite is brass-colored and often mistaken for gold, but its streak is black (gold makes a gold streak). Spinel crystals can be red, blue, brown, green, purple, white, or black, but they all have a white streak. If the mineral is very hard, use a steel file to remove some powder, and this powder will show you the mineral's color.

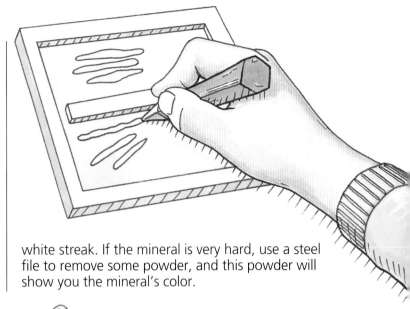

3 Measuring specific gravity

A one-inch cube of gold weighs more than a one-inch cube of quartz. Why? Gold has a higher density—that is, more matter tightly packed into the same amount of space. Specific gravity is a way to measure density by comparing the weight of a mineral to the weight of the same volume of water. Water's specific gravity is 1—gold's is 19.3. Given an equal volume of water and of gold, the gold will weigh 19.3 times more than the water. To measure specific gravity using this method, you need a hanging scale with a hook (you can buy one in a hardware store).

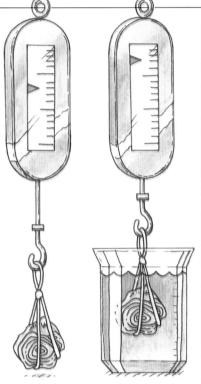

1 **Tie the mineral up in a sling** and weigh it dry (see left-hand picture). Write the weight (**A**).
2 **Put a glass or jar of water under the scale**.
3 **Hang the mineral** in the water in the sling (see right-hand picture).
4 **Write down the weight** of the mineral in the water (**B**).
5 **Work out the specific gravity** this way: **A** (weight in air) minus **B** (weight in water) equals volume (**C**). **A** (weight in air) divided by volume (**C**) equals specific gravity.

Igneous Minerals

Analcime

Analcime is found as a secondary mineral in many igneous rocks. Its crystals are transparent or translucent. They may be colorless, white, gray, or have pink, green, or yellow tinges. Analcime is found all over the world. Large crystals have been found in Nova Scotia, Canada. Locations of other notable deposits include Colorado, Michigan, and New Jersey in the United States and Italy, Germany, and Scotland in Europe. The mineral's name comes from Greek words meaning "not strong," because when the crystal is heated or rubbed it develops a weak electric charge.

Chemical composition: $NaAlSi_2O_6 \cdot H_2O$
Crystal system: Isometric
Hardness: 5–5.5—Specific gravity: 2.22–2.3—Streak: White

Apophyllite

Apophyllite is a secondary mineral in basalt and other igneous rocks. In the United States, its glassy crystals may be found in such states as Michigan, New Jersey, Oregon, and Virginia. Pale pink or white crystals have been found in Mexico. Beautiful green crystals come from India. Apophyllite crystals may also be colorless, gray, or yellowish. The name apophyllite comes from Greek words meaning "to strip leaves," because the mineral flakes into pieces when heated.

Chemical composition: $KCa_4Si_8O_{20}(F,OH) \cdot 8H_2O$
Crystal system: Tetragonal
Hardness: 4.5–5—Specific gravity: 2.3–2.5—Streak: White

Copper

Copper is one of the most useful metals. It is found in ores combined with sulfur, and more rarely as a native (pure) metal. The finest native copper comes from the Keeweenaw Peninsula on Lake Superior. Copper is easily shaped by being drawn into threads or beaten, and it is an excellent conductor of electricity and heat. In ancient times, a source of copper was Cyprus, an island in the northeast of the Mediterranean Sea. Copper's name and symbol come from *cuprum*, the Roman name for the Cyprian metal.

Chemical composition: Cu
Crystal system: Isometric
Hardness: 2.5–3—Specific gravity: 8.9—Streak: Red

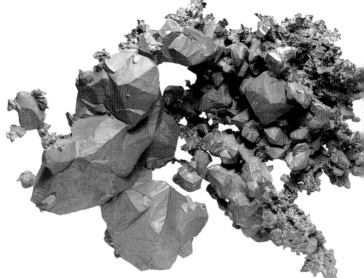

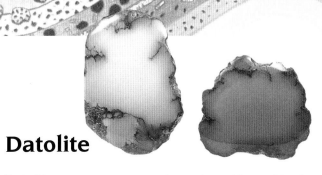

Datolite

Datolite occurs as a secondary mineral in cavities in basalt, granite, and other igneous rocks. It comes in many transparent or translucent colors, from red through pink, brown, yellow, and green to white and colorless. In the United States, there are major deposits in New Jersey and Massachusetts. Datolite crystals occur in native copper deposits near Lake Superior in Michigan state and in some silver mines in Mexico. The name comes from a Greek word meaning "to divide." Datolite is a source of the element boron. Large crystals are occasionally used as gemstones.

Chemical composition: $CaBSiO_4(OH)$
Crystal system: Monoclinic
Hardness: 5–5.5—Specific gravity: 2.8–3
Streak: Colorless

Diamond

Diamond is the hardest naturally occurring substance. It may be colorless, yellow, green, blue, or pink. It is found in pipe-shaped deposits of a rock called kimberlite. These pipes are rock formations that filled and hardened in the vents of certain volcanoes. Diamond has also been found in gravel and sand deposits of stream beds. The main sources are Australia, southern and western Africa, and Russia. Diamond is almost entirely carbon. Its name comes from a Greek word meaning "hardest metal." The finest stones are used as jewelry. Tiny diamonds are used in industry for cutting and drilling.

Chemical composition: C
Crystal system: Isometric
Hardness: 10
Specific gravity: 3.5
Streak: White

Magnetite

Magnetite is an important source of iron. It is black and magnetic, and it sometimes forms a lodestone (a natural magnet). Magnetite is found all over the world in igneous, sedimentary, and metamorphic rocks. The most powerful lodestones are found today in Russia, on the Italian Island of Elba in the Mediterranean Sea, and in South Africa. The name magnetite comes from Magnesia, a district in western Asia Minor, where the mineral was mined in ancient times.

Chemical composition: Fe_3O_4
Crystal system: Isometric
Hardness: 5.5–6.5—Specific gravity: 4.9–5.2—Streak: Black

Natrolite

Natrolite is found in cavities in basalt and other igneous rocks. Its slender, square needlelike crystals are colorless or white. Huge crystals have been found at Asbestos in southern Quebec, and at Bound Brook, New Jersey. Very large crystals have also been found in Russia. Natrolite's name comes from the Greek word *natron* (sodium), its main ingredient.

Chemical composition: $Na_2Al_2Si_3O_{10}\cdot 2H_2O$
Crystal system: Orthorhombic
Hardness: 5–5.5—Specific gravity: 2.2–2.3—Streak: White

Igneous Minerals

Olivine

Olivine is the name of a group of minerals that are compounds of silicon, magnesium, and iron. They range from forsterite (magnesium silicate) to fayalite (iron silicate). The clear green variety of olivine, called peridot, is valued as a gemstone. Olivines are found all over the world in igneous rocks. Their name comes from the olive-green color typical of many varieties. Since ancient times, the finest peridot has come from Jazirat Zabarjat (St. John's Island) off the Egyptian coast in the Red Sea. In the United States, Arizona and New Mexico are important sources for the gem.

Chemical composition: Mg_2SiO_4 to Fe_2SiO_4
Crystal system: Orthorhombic
Hardness: 6.5–7
Specific gravity: 3.2–4.4; peridot approximately 3.2–3.3
Streak: White or colorless

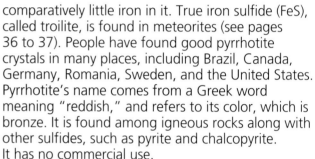

Pyrrhotite

Pyrrhotite is a form of iron sulfide, but with comparatively little iron in it. True iron sulfide (FeS), called troilite, is found in meteorites (see pages 36 to 37). People have found good pyrrhotite crystals in many places, including Brazil, Canada, Germany, Romania, Sweden, and the United States. Pyrrhotite's name comes from a Greek word meaning "reddish," and refers to its color, which is bronze. It is found among igneous rocks along with other sulfides, such as pyrite and chalcopyrite. It has no commercial use.

Chemical composition: $Fe_{1-x}S$ (x=0 to 0.2)
Crystal system: Monoclinic and hexagonal
Hardness: 3.5–4.5—Specific gravity: 4.5–4.7
Streak: Dark grayish-black

Sodalite

Sodalite is found in igneous rocks (such as syenite), and in volcanic rocks and altered limestones. Sodalite varies from colorless to dark blue, occasionally white, yellowish, reddish, or greenish. Beautiful blue sodalite has been found in Ontario and British Columbia in Canada. Other places where sodalite is found include South Africa, Brazil, and in the lava flows of Vesuvius and other Italian volcanoes. Large masses are used as polished slabs or for carving. Its name comes from its main ingredient, sodium.

Chemical composition:
$Na_8Al_6Si_6O_{24}Cl_2$
Crystal system:
Isometric
Hardness: 5.5–6
Specific gravity:
2.2–2.4
Streak: Colorless

Zircon

Zircon is a gemstone with a wide range of colors, stretching from colorless (when it has been used as a substitute for diamond) through yellow, brown, red, and green. Zircons are found throughout the world in granites or in alluvial (river) deposits. The best gem-quality stones come from Southeast Asia, especially Cambodia, Myanmar, and Thailand. Australia, France, Norway, and Sri Lanka are also major sources of gem-quality stones. The name is derived through Arabic from a Persian word meaning "gold-colored."

Chemical composition: $ZrSiO_4$
Crystal system: Tetragonal
Hardness: 7.5—Specific gravity: 4.6–4.7—Streak: White

The minerals on pages 49 to 51 are secondary minerals, often found near hot springs.

Arsenopyrite

Arsenopyrite is iron arsenic sulfide. It is the main source of the poisonous chemical element arsenic, which has several industrial uses. If you hit lumps of arsenopyrite with a hammer (wear protective eyegear), they give off a smell like garlic. Arsenopyrite is found worldwide in veins in metal mines, especially with gold, nickel, silver, and tin. Many gold-bearing veins in the Sierra Nevada of California contain arsenopyrite. Some European locations known for good crystals include Cornwall in England, and Germany. Its name comes from its ingredients.
Chemical composition: FeAsS
Crystal system: Monoclinic
Hardness: 5.5–6—Specific gravity: 5.9–6.2
Streak: Black or dark gray

Bournonite

Bournonite is an ore of antimony, copper, and lead, which are its main ingredients. It is black to very dark gray, with a metallic luster. It is common and is found in hydrothermal veins, often with galena, quartz, and other minerals. Large crystals have been found at Park City, Utah, and in several other western states in the United States. Other sources include Mexico, Cornwall in England, Germany, and Japan. Crystals up to 4 inches (10 centimeters) across have come from Bolivia. It is named for the French crystallographer Count Jacques Louis de Bournon.
Chemical composition: PbCuSbS$_3$—Crystal system: Orthorhombic
Hardness: 2.5–3—Specific gravity: 5.8–5.9
Streak: Steel-gray to black

Cassiterite

Cassiterite is tin oxide, and it is the principal ore of tin. It usually occurs in veins associated with quartz. It is found as crystals or as masses in or near granite. The major producers of cassiterite include Brazil, Bolivia, China, Indonesia, and Malaysia. There is very little in the United States. The name comes from the Greek word for tin.

Chemical composition: SnO$_2$
Crystal system: Tetragonal
Hardness: 6–7
Specific gravity: 6.8–7.1
Streak: White or brownish

Galena

Galena is the chief ore of lead, and it often occurs in association with silver. It forms brittle, gray isometric crystals, easily identified. Galena is found throughout the world, in widely differing types of deposits—including limestones and hydrothermal veins. Fine specimens come from the area around Joplin, Missouri, and nearby parts of Kansas and Oklahoma in the United States. The main commercial sources are in Australia, Canada, China, Mexico, Peru, and the United States. The name comes from the Latin word for lead ore.
Chemical composition: PbS—Crystal system: Isometric
Hardness: 2.5–2.75—Specific gravity: 2.4–2.6—Streak: Gray

Igneous Minerals

Gold

Gold is a soft metal. It is valued because it does not rust or tarnish. It is the most malleable metal—it can be easily hammered or pressed into any shape the goldsmith desires. Gold can also be drawn into fine wires without breaking. It is most familiar in the form of a native metal—grains or nuggets. Its color is golden-yellow. It may look paler if mixed with silver or nickel and reddish-gold if mixed with copper. It is found in hydrothermal veins, near volcanic vents, or in river beds. The leading gold-mining countries are South Africa, the United States, Australia, China, and Canada. The name "gold" comes from the Latin word "shining dawn."

Chemical composition: Au
Crystal system: Isometric
Hardness: 2.5–3
Specific gravity: 19.3
Streaks: Same as the color of the nugget

Pectolite

Pectolite is found in cavities in basalt and other igneous rocks. It is usually colorless, white, or gray. It often forms needlelike crystals which can prick when touched. Good, pale crystals are found in New Jersey in the United States, and in Quebec and Ontario in Canada. Other sources include Italy and the Kola Peninsula in Russia. A deeper blue variety from the Dominican Republic, called Larimar, is used as an ornamental stone, but pectolite has no other uses. Its name comes from a Greek word meaning "compact," because it is compact in structure.

Chemical composition: $NaCa_2Si_3O_8(OH)$
Crystal system: Triclinic
Hardness: 4.5–5—Specific gravity: 2.7–2.9— Streak: White

Prehnite

Prehnite is found in cavities and veins in igneous rocks such as basalt and granite, in the metamorphic rock gneiss, and in metamorphosed limestones. It is named for the Dutch soldier Colonel Hendrik van Prehn, who first collected it in South Africa in the 1700's. Prehnite is often green, but may be gray, yellowish, white, or colorless. Locations where fine crystals can be found include New Jersey and Virginia in the United States, Quebec in Canada, France, and South Africa.

Chemical composition: $Ca_2Al_2Si_3O_{10}(OH)_2$
Crystal system: Orthorhombic
Hardness: 6–6.5—Specific gravity: 2.9–3—Streak: Colorless

Siderite

Siderite is iron carbonate. It is nearly half iron, and is an important ore for that metal. It is a common mineral, with worldwide distribution. Its transparent to translucent crystals are brown, greenish, gray, or white. It occurs in many rock formations, including sedimentary layers (along with coal seams), hydrothermal veins, and basaltic rocks. Places in the United States with good crystals include Colorado and New England. Other locations worldwide include Greenland, England, Austria, Portugal, and Brazil. Its name comes from the Greek word meaning "iron."

Chemical composition: $FeCO_3$—Crystal system: Rhombohedral
Hardness: 3.5–4.5—Specific gravity: 3.8–3.9—Streak: White

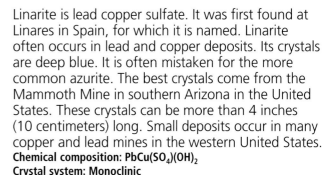

Linarite

Linarite is lead copper sulfate. It was first found at Linares in Spain, for which it is named. Linarite often occurs in lead and copper deposits. Its crystals are deep blue. It is often mistaken for the more common azurite. The best crystals come from the Mammoth Mine in southern Arizona in the United States. These crystals can be more than 4 inches (10 centimeters) long. Small deposits occur in many copper and lead mines in the western United States.

Chemical composition: $PbCu(SO_4)(OH)_2$
Crystal system: Monoclinic
Hardness: 2.5—Specific gravity: 5.3–5.4—Streak: Pale blue

Stibnite

Stibnite is antimony sulfide, and it is the most important ore of the chemical element antimony. Stibnite forms lead-gray, slender metallic crystals, which are much sought after by collectors. It occurs in hydrothermal veins and in hot springs. The finest crystals came from the Ichinokawa mines in Japan, but these are now almost worked out. Other important sources for fine crystals include China, Peru, and Romania. In the United States, some of the best crystals come from Nevada. The name comes from the Greek word for antimony. The ancient Egyptians, Greeks, and Romans used powdered stibnite as eye makeup.

Chemical composition: Sb_2S_3
Crystal system: Orthorhombic
Hardness: 2
Specific gravity: 4.6
Streak: Dark gray

Witherite

Witherite occurs in hydrothermal veins, often with barite and galena. It forms white or gray translucent crystals, sometimes tinged with green or brown. Though fairly rare, it is found in lead mines in parts of England; and in the United States in fluorite mines in Illinois and lead mines in Arizona. Witherite is an important source of barium, which, when combined with other chemicals, has many uses in industry. It is named for an English physician, William Withering, who first described it in the 1700's.

Chemical composition: $BaCO_3$
Crystal system: Orthorhombic
Hardness: 3–3.5
Specific gravity: 4.3
Streak: White

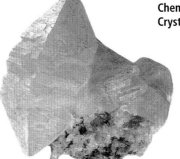

Igneous Minerals

The minerals on these two pages are often found with sulfur deposits or near salt lakes.

Argentite

Argentite is silver sulfide, and it is a major ore of silver. Its name comes from the Latin word for silver. It is often found with native silver and galena. There was a major deposit in the Comstock Lode in Nevada in the United States, and it is also found in several other western states. Other sources of fine crystals include Mexico, Germany, Norway, and Canada (especially Ontario and British Columbia). Argentite crystallizes only above 355 °F (179 °C). At normal temperatures it occurs in a chemically identical form called acanthite.

Chemical composition: Ag_2S—Crystal system: Isometric
Hardness: 2–2.5—Specific gravity: 7.2–7.4—Streak: Shiny black

Chalcocite

Chalcocite is an important source of copper and is found with other copper minerals. The most common form of chalcocite is large, dull gray aggregates. The individual shiny gray crystals are rare, but some fine ones have been found in the United States in Bristol, Connecticut, and Butte, Montana; they are also found in Cornwall, England. Chalcocite is mined in many parts of the western United States. Its name comes from the Greek word for copper.

Chemical composition: CU_2S—Crystal system: Orthorhombic
Hardness: 2.5–3—Specific gravity: 5.5–5.8
Streak: Blackish lead-gray

Barite

Barite is a very heavy mineral; another name for it is heavy spar. (The weight of a specimen is a good clue to identifying it.) Barite is the most common ore of barium. It is found worldwide in hydrothermal veins or in limestone and other sedimentary rocks. It can be colorless, white, yellow-brown, red, or blue, and it is transparent or translucent. Gem-quality yellow crystals are mined in the United States in South Dakota. Huge crystals have been mined in England. Crystal growths containing barite, called desert roses, occur in such dry regions as the Sahara in Africa and the Great Basin in the western United States. The name comes from a Greek word meaning "heavy."

Chemical composition: $BaSO_4$—Crystal system: Orthorhombic
Hardness: 3–3.5—Specific gravity: 4.3–4.6—Streak: White

Chalcopyrite

Chalcopyrite is a copper iron sulfide, and it is the most common copper mineral. It is brassy yellow in color, but tarnishes. It is found with other sulfide deposits, often in hydrothermal veins (those created by high temperatures and water). Major deposits occur in Canada, Japan, Spain, and the United States. The major United States deposits are in Arizona, Montana, Tennessee, and Utah. The name comes from two Greek words meaning "copper" and "fiery."

Chemical composition: $CuFeS_2$
Crystal system: Tetragonal
Hardness: 3.5–4
Specific gravity: 4.1–4.3
Streak: Greenish-black

Cinnabar

Cinnabar consists of mercury and sulfur. It is the main source of mercury, which is the only metal that is liquid at room temperature. Cinnabar usually forms red, gray, or black masses, but also is found as scarlet crystals. It is commonly found in veins near recently formed volcanic rocks. In Spain, mines begun by the ancient Romans still produce cinnabar. Deposits also occur in China, Italy, Slovenia, and Spain; and in California, Nevada, and Oregon in the United States. The name comes from the Persian word for this mineral.

Chemical composition: HgS
Crystal system: Hexagonal or rhombohedral
Hardness: 2–2.5
Specific gravity: 8.1
Streak: Scarlet to reddish-brown

Colemanite

Colemanite is one of the main ores of the chemical element boron. It forms colorless or white crystals, and also masses. Colemanite is found in salt-lake deposits. It is extensively mined in California, especially in Death Valley, and also in Argentina, Chile, Kazakhstan, and Turkey. Boron is used in the chemical industry and in nuclear reactors. Colemanite is named for William Tell Coleman, one of the founders of the American borax industry.

Chemical composition:
$Ca_2B_6O_{11} \cdot 5H_2O$
Crystal system: Monoclinic
Hardness: 4–4.5
Specific gravity: 2.4
Streak: White

Gypsum

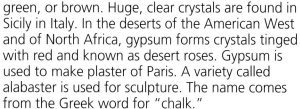

Gypsum is formed through the evaporation of salty water and often occurs in sedimentary deposits. It also occurs near hot springs or volcanoes. It is found in many parts of the world. It forms crystals of various shapes, colorless or white to pale yellow, green, or brown. Huge, clear crystals are found in Sicily in Italy. In the deserts of the American West and of North Africa, gypsum forms crystals tinged with red and known as desert roses. Gypsum is used to make plaster of Paris. A variety called alabaster is used for sculpture. The name comes from the Greek word for "chalk."

Chemical composition: $CaSO_4 \cdot 2H_2O$
Crystal system: Monoclinic
Hardness: 2—Specific gravity: 2.3—Streak: White

Sulfur

Sulfur is one of the chemical elements that occurs in a native state (that is, not mixed with other minerals). It often occurs as a result of volcanic activity, as at the volcanic vents in Yellowstone National Park in the United States and also on the slopes of Mount Vesuvius in Italy. There are large sulfur beds in the United States in Louisiana and Texas. It forms beautiful yellow crystals, which are transparent or translucent. The finest crystals are found at Agrigento, Sicily. Sulfur's name comes from the Latin word for this element.

Chemical composition: S—Crystal system: Orthorhombic
Hardness: 1.5–2.5—Specific gravity: 2–2.1—Streak: White

Igneous Minerals

All the minerals described on the next four pages are usually found with a granite called pegmatite (see page 13).

Apatite

Apatite is the name of a group of common phosphate, arsenate, and vanadate minerals. The most common is chlorapatite, which is basically made up of calcium phosphate with chlorine. Apatite is found in volcanic and other igneous rocks, some sedimentary rocks, and in metamorphic rocks. It varies from colorless or white to yellow, brown, green, blue, or red. It is used in the chemical industry. Some fine crystals are used as gemstones, including violet crystals from Germany, blue crystals from Maine in the United States, and yellow ones from Mexico. The name comes from a Greek word meaning "deceit," because apatite was commonly confused with other minerals.

Chemical composition: $Ca_5(PO_4)_3(F \cdot Cl \cdot OH)$ and variations
Crystal system: Hexagonal
Hardness: 5—Specific gravity: 3.1–3.2—Streak: White

Beryl

Beryl is made of beryllium, aluminum, silicon, and oxygen. It occurs worldwide in the igneous rock pegmatite. Pure beryl, called goshenite, is colorless. Varieties of beryl include the gemstones aquamarine, which is colored blue by traces of iron, and emerald, which is colored green by chromium. The finest emeralds come from Colombia and the most important source of aquamarines is Brazil. Traces of manganese give color to deep red bixbite from Utah in the United States and to pink beryl, called morganite, which is found, among other places, in California. Iron in another form makes the beryl called heliodor yellow. Beryl crystals can weigh up to several tons. It is the main source of beryllium, used in rockets and missiles. The name comes from the Greek name for the mineral.

Chemical composition: $Be_3Al_2Si_6O_{18}$
Crystal system: Hexagonal
Hardness: 7.5–8—Specific gravity: 2.6–2.9—Streak: White

Biotite

Biotite is one of a group of minerals called micas. It occurs worldwide in granites, pegmatites, gabbros, schists, gneisses, and other igneous or metamorphic rocks. It forms black, brown, or dark green crystals but is normally found in plates or sheets. It is one of the most common and important rock-forming minerals. Good crystals are found in New England in the United States and Quebec and Ontario in Canada. It is named for a French physicist of the 1800's, Jean Baptiste Biot.

Chemical composition: $K(Mg,O_{10}Fe)_3(Al,Fe)Si_3O_{10}(OH,F)_2$
Crystal system: Monoclinic
Hardness: 2.5–3—Specific gravity: 2.8–3.4—Streak: Colorless

Ilmenite

Ilmenite is iron titanium oxide. It is one of the principal ores of the metal titanium. Ilmenite occurs as aggregates, or as flat black to dark brown crystals. It is often found in pegmatites, volcanic rocks, and metamorphic rocks. Weathering and wave action have deposited it as black sands in such places as Florida in the United States, Western Australia, and South Africa. Other places ilmenite occurs include Quebec, Canada, and Iron Mountain, Wyoming, in the United States. It is named for the Ilmen Mountains in Russia.

Chemical composition: $FeTiO_3$
Crystal system: Rhombohedral
Hardness: 5–6—Specific gravity: 4.1–4.8
Streak: Black to yellow or brownish-red

Microcline

Microcline is potassium aluminum silicate and is one of the potassium group of feldspar minerals. It forms crystals colored white, pink, red, yellow, or green. Microcline occurs worldwide in pegmatites, schists, and granites. A green variety, amazonite, is cut and polished as a gemstone. One place it is found is Pike's Peak, Colorado, in the United States. The name comes from two Greek words meaning "small slant," because these triclinic crystals contain no right angles.

Chemical composition: $KAlSi_3O_8$
Crystal system: Triclinic
Hardness: 6–6.5—Specific gravity: 2.4–2.6—Streak: White

Igneous Minerals

Monazite

Monazite is a phosphate of the radioactive element thorium and of several of the elements known as rare earths. It is the principal ore of thorium and cerium. It forms yellow to brown crystals that are most commonly found in granites, gneisses, schists, and sands formed by the weathering of those rocks. Brazil and India have major deposits. The name comes from a Greek word meaning "solitary," and refers to the mineral's rarity.

Chemical composition: $(Ce,La,Y,Th)PO_4$
Crystal system: Monoclinic
Hardness: 5–5.5—Specific gravity: 4.6–5.4
Streak: White

Muscovite

Muscovite is the most common of the mica minerals. It occurs worldwide in igneous and metamorphic rocks and sandstones. Huge crystals occur occasionally. One crystal found in India weighed about 85 tons (75 metric tons). The crystals are transparent or translucent, and range from colorless through gray, brown, yellow, green, violet, and rose to ruby-red. It is used to make heat and electrical insulation, paper, paint, and porcelain. It is named for Russians or "Muscovites," who once used the material as window glass.

Chemical composition:
$KAl_3Si_3O_{10}(OH,F)_2$
Crystal system: Monoclinic
Hardness: 2.5–3
Specific gravity: 2.7–3
Streak: Colorless

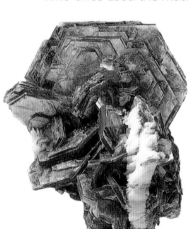

Orthoclase

Orthoclase is potassium aluminum silicate. Like microcline, it is one of the feldspar minerals, but it generally crystallizes at a hotter temperature than microcline and forms differently shaped crystals. It occurs worldwide, particularly in pegmatites. Its crystals are mostly colorless or white, but they may be pale shades of gray, yellow, pink, or blue. It occurs widely in the western United States. Unusual yellow crystals come from Madagascar. A variety containing thin plates of ablite (a sodium-rich feldspar) forms the gemstone called moonstone. Locations where orthoclase is found include New Mexico and Virginia in the United States, Myanmar, and Sri Lanka. Orthoclase has many industrial uses, for example as a scouring powder. The name comes from two Greek words meaning "straight fracture," because the crystals cleave at right angles.

Chemical composition: $KAlSi_3O_8$—Crystal system: Monoclinic
Hardness: 6—Specific gravity: 2.5–2.6—Streak: White

Rutile

Rutile is titanium oxide; an important ore of the metal titanium. It occurs in many different environments, including pegmatites, hydrothermal veins, sediments, placer (river) deposits, and sands. Fine crystals are found in the United States at Graves Mountain, Georgia, and in Virginia. Rutile also occurs in the Alps in Europe, and in Australia and Brazil. The mineral ranges from reddish-brown through red and yellow to black. It usually has a solid, metallic look or translucent appearance. The name comes from a Latin word meaning "reddish."

Chemical composition: TiO_2—Crystal system: Tetragonal
Hardness: 6–6.5—Specific gravity: 4.2–4.3
Streak: Pale brown to yellowish

Spodumene

Spodumene is lithium aluminum silicate, and it is one of the pyroxene group of minerals. It is frequently found in granite pegmatites. It forms crystals varying from colorless through yellow, pink, and green to violet. Some crystals found in South Dakota are huge, more than 50 feet (15 meters) long. Spodumene is also found in the United States in Connecticut, Maine, Massachusetts, and New Mexico. Deposits also occur in Sweden, Madagascar, Brazil, and Mexico. Gem varieties of spodumene occur in several colors, including lilac (called kunzite), yellow, and emerald-green (called hiddenite, which is found only in the United States in North Carolina). Spodumene is a source of lithium. Its name comes from a Greek word meaning "reduced to ashes," referring to its pale color.

Chemical composition: $LiAlSi_2O_6$
Crystal system: Monoclinic
Hardness: 6.5–7.5—Specific gravity: 3–3.2—Streak: White

Tourmaline

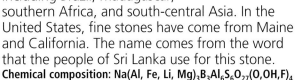

Tourmaline is the name of a group of minerals with a complex composition based on boron, aluminum, and silica. Tourmaline forms in igneous and metamorphic rocks, particularly granite pegmatites. There are six main varieties. Most gem tourmaline is elbaite, with the chemical composition as given below, or liddicoatite. Tourmaline comes in all colors, from clear to black. Some crystals are more than one color, for example, green at one end and red at the other. Tourmalines are found in many places, including Brazil, Madagascar, southern Africa, and south-central Asia. In the United States, fine stones have come from Maine and California. The name comes from the word that the people of Sri Lanka use for this stone.

Chemical composition: $Na(Al, Fe, Li, Mg)_3B_3Al_6Si_6O_{27}(O,OH,F)_4$ (Elbaite)
Crystal system: Hexagonal
Hardness: 7–7.5—Specific gravity: 3–3.3—Streak: Colorless

Topaz

Topaz, a mineral that most often occurs in granite pegmatites, is best known as a gemstone. Its crystals vary in color and may be colorless to white, yellow, pink, red, or blue. Yellow-orange topaz, called imperial topaz, is the most valuable. The finest imperial topaz comes from Brazil.

The other major sources of topaz include Australia, Brazil, Namibia, Nigeria, Pakistan, and Russia. Other yellow stones, such as citrine (see quartz), are often passed off as topaz. The name comes from the Greek word for the gem.

Chemical composition: $Al_2SiO_4(FOH)_2$
Crystal system: Orthorhombic
Hardness: 8
Specific gravity: 3.5–3.6
Streak: Colorless

Collecting Specimens

There is no better way to study rocks and minerals than to collect them. But, that means you must collect as many specimens as possible in the field, rather than buy from your local rock store. You can't really learn about a rock unless you see where it comes from.

If possible, always go with somebody who knows about rocks and minerals, like a teacher or an experienced collector. They can tell you what you are looking at. You can also join your local mineral society. Belonging to such a group is a good way to learn in the field.

Where to go hunting

Your work begins at home, by studying maps and guides to locate good collecting sites. The best map is a geological map, with bright colors to show you the location of the various types of rocks.

Find out where there are old mine dumps. These often have rock specimens taken from underground. Beaches are another good hunting place. **But always ask permission before exploring, especially on property that may be private. And always tell a responsible adult where you are going.**

Recording your finds

Try to find loose specimens on the ground—don't break new lumps off the existing rock. Remember that a weathered specimen won't show clearly what the rock is, so be prepared to break the specimen to get an unweathered face to examine.

As soon as you have found a specimen, write down in your notebook where you found it and what you think it is. Then put the specimen in a

plastic bag, together with a brief description on a piece of paper, and seal it. (It is better not to write on the bag itself—your writing might rub off.) You can also number the bag and record details about the specimen in your notebook. **This is important**—if you don't describe where a specimen comes from, it is useless later to anyone studying rocks and minerals.

It's a good idea to take photographs of the sites where you find your specimens. If you are taking a close-up of a crystal, always include something in the picture to give an idea of its size—a pencil or a small ruler will do.

Minerals you are most likely to find in the field include opaque quartz varieties (page 69), pyrite (page 69), and small garnets (page 72). Leave them embedded in the rock where you found them—don't try to pry them out or you will damage the formations.

What you need

To do your collecting properly you will need some simple equipment, but it must be the right gear. This is what you will need in the field.

1 **Footwear:** walking boots are the best; loose rocks can move, and some are sharp. Strong sneakers (laced up properly) can also protect your feet and ankles against injury.
2 **Clothes:** in hot weather make sure you have light clothes that will also protect you from sunburn. In cooler weather, jeans, a sweater (and waterproof clothes if rain is likely) are best. You also need gloves to protect your hands.
3 **A lightweight backpack:** for your specimens. A backpack leaves your hands free.
4 **A hardhat or other protective head gear:** rockfalls sometimes occur on the cliff faces under which some of the best specimens appear.
5 **Small self-sealing plastic bags:** to put your specimens in.

6 **A roll of 1.5- by 3-inch (4- by 12-centimeter) self-adhesive labels:** these are easier to use for notes about your specimens instead of writing on the bag itself.
7 **A trowel:** for digging specimens out of earth. But don't use it to pry specimens out of the rock—you may damage vital mineral groups or fossil specimens. You can find unweathered, loose material very easily on most sites if you hunt around a little.
8 **A small magnifying glass:** buy one that is 10 power (labeled X 10), and wear it on a cord round your neck. A rock store will have one. To use it, hold the glass close to your eye and then bring the specimen close to the glass.
9 **A field notebook with pencils and pens:** you'll need a pen or pencil to take notes on both the specimens you find and the location in which you found them.
10 **A camera:** if you take photographs of crystals and rock formations, rather than prying them out of the rock matrix, it avoids damaging the environment.

Sedimentary Minerals

Celestite

Celestite is a heavy mineral usually found in sedimentary rocks, especially limestones. It sometimes occurs in igneous rocks or hydrothermal veins. The crystals are translucent or transparent. Some are colorless or white. Others are pale blue—its name comes from an Italian word which means "skylike." Places in the United States with excellent crystals include Ohio, Colorado, and New York. Other locations include England, Italy, and Madagascar. Celestite is the main ore of strontium.

Chemical composition: $SrSO_4$
Crystal system: Orthorhombic
Hardness: 3–3.5
Specific gravity: 3.9–4.0—Streak: White

Hematite

Hematite is the chief ore of iron. It occurs most commonly in thick sedimentary beds, which are found in many parts of the world. One of the largest beds is near Lake Superior in Michigan, Minnesota, and Wisconsin. Some hematite forms in volcanic rocks. Hematite is gray to black in color, but when exposed to oxygen it turns red—it is this reaction that causes the reddish rust that forms on iron. Hematite also occurs as crystals or sometimes as thin flakes forming rosettes. Countries with large deposits include Australia, Brazil, Canada, South Africa, and the United States. The name hematite comes from the Greek word for blood.

Chemical composition: Fe_2O_3—Crystal system: Rhombohedral
Hardness: 5–6—Specific gravity: 4.9–5.3—Streak: Deep red

Halite

Halite is the mineral name for common salt. It provides beautiful isometric crystals and large masses, but it dissolves in water. Halite is usually colorless but may be tinged with blue, red, or yellow. It occurs as sedimentary deposits, resulting from the evaporation of ancient oceans or salt lakes. Deposits are widespread. There are huge layers of halite deep beneath the Mediterranean and Red seas. In the United States, Louisiana, Texas, and New York produce the most salt. Ontario produces most of Canada's salt. The other major salt-producing countries include China, Germany, India, and Australia. We use salt in our food, and it is added to packaged foods—sometimes for flavor and sometimes as a preservative. The name halite comes from the Greek word for salt.

Chemical composition: NaCl – Crystal system: Isometric
Hardness: 2.5—Specific gravity: 2.16—Streak: Colorless or white

Jadeite

Jadeite is sodium aluminum silicate. It is the harder, more brilliantly colored of the two minerals known as jade. The other mineral called jade is nephrite. Most jadeite is found as pebbles or boulders in streams. Jade has been prized by Chinese jewelers and carvers for thousands of years. The finest, so-called imperial jade, is a bright emerald-green, but jadeite can also be gray, lavender, yellow, or reddish-brown. Most jadeite comes from Myanmar, Japan, and California. Its name comes from a Spanish phrase meaning "stone of the side," because it was believed to cure pains in the kidneys if applied to the side of the body.
Chemical composition: $NaAl,Si_2O_6$
Crystal system: Monoclinic
Hardness: 6.5–7— Specific gravity: 3.3–3.5
Streak: Colorless

Platinum

Platinum is one of the main precious metals, along with gold and silver. Platinum is found as a native element, meaning it is not combined with other minerals. Platinum minerals often occur along with gold minerals in placer deposits, these having been washed out of igneous rocks. Platinum is rarely found as nuggets or crystals; it is mostly found in grains or plates. Today, most platinum comes from South Africa, Russia, and Canada. The United States and Colombia also produce large amounts. Used in jewelry and precision instruments, its name comes from the Spanish word meaning "silver."
Chemical composition: Pt—Crystal system: Isometric
Hardness: 4–4.5—Specific gravity: 14–19
Streak: Silvery-white

Nephrite

Nephrite is the other mineral which is described as jade. It is more common and less valuable than jadeite. It is a silicate formed with calcium magnesium or calcium iron and ranges in color from white, yellow, and gray to red, dark green, and black. Nephrite was the main mineral used by the ancient Chinese for carving. Their nephrite came from Turkestan, but most nephrite today is mined in New Zealand. Its name comes from the Greek word meaning "kidney," because people once thought amulets made of nephrite or jadeite could prevent kidney stones.
Chemical composition: $Ca_2(Mg,Fe)_5Si_8O_{22}(OH)_2$
Crystal system: Monoclinic
Hardness: 6–6.5—Specific gravity: about 3—Streak: White

Turquoise

Turquoise is a blue to blue-green mineral formed when water slowly causes chemical changes in surface rocks that contain aluminum. The blue-green color comes from traces of copper. Turquoise usually forms in very dry regions. Major sources are Iran, Tibet, and the southwestern United States, especially Colorado, Nevada, and New Mexico. It occurs mostly as masses, often in rock cavities, but crystals are rare. The name comes from an old French word meaning "Turkish," because turquoise was originally imported into Europe through Turkey.
Chemical composition:
$CuAl_6(PO_4)_4(OH)_8 \cdot 4H_2O$
Crystal system: Triclinic
Hardness: 5–6
Specific gravity: 2.6–2.8
Streak: White to pale green

Secondary Minerals

All the minerals shown on pages 62 to 69 are secondary minerals, which means that they have been changed by chemical reactions within their original rocks and not by movements of the earth's crust.

Anglesite

Anglesite is found in lead ore as a secondary mineral. It is formed by the oxidation of galena. Crystals are usually colorless or white, but they may be pale gray, green, blue, or red. Anglesite is mined for its lead content when found in large concentrations. Places where it occurs include Mexico and much of the western United States. Anglesite is named for the island of Anglesey, off the northwest corner of Wales, where the mineral was originally identified.

Chemical composition: $PbSO_4$
Crystal system: Orthorhombic
Hardness: 2.5–3
Specific gravity: 6.4
Streak: Colorless to white

Cerussite

Cerussite is lead carbonate and is a secondary mineral that forms when the upper layers of lead ore deposits are oxidized by water containing carbonic acid. The crystals of cerussite are colorless or yellow, sometimes tinged with other colors by impurities. It is abundant in lead mines in North America. Some of the best crystals come from Australia, Morocco, Namibia, and New Zealand. Cerussite is used as a lead ore, though some crystals are cut as gemstones. The name comes from the Latin name meaning "lead carbonate."

Chemical composition: $PbCO_3$
Crystal system: Orthorhombic
Hardness: 3–3.5
Specific gravity: 6.5–6.6
Streak: White

Azurite

Azurite is a deep blue mineral found in copper deposits. It forms large crystals, rosettes or, more rarely, masses. It is often found with malachite. Azurite is sometimes mined for its copper content, but it is usually used to make jewelry and decorative objects. The best crystals are found near Lyon in France. Fine azurite also comes from Australia, Greece, Mexico, Namibia, Romania, Russia, and the United States. Its name comes from the Old French word for "blue."

Chemical composition: $Cu_3(CO_3)_2(OH)_2$
Crystal system: Monoclinic
Hardness: 3.5–4—Specific gravity: 3.7–3.8—Streak: Blue

Chalcanthite

Chalcanthite is hydrated copper sulfate, a secondary mineral of copper. The color of its crystals ranges from sky-blue to deep blue. Chalcanthite is found only in dry areas because it dissolves in water. It may crystallize in a damp mine, forming crusts or stalactites. Chalcanthite goes powdery when very dry. It is found in copper

mines in the western United States. The biggest deposits are in Chile, where it is a major copper ore, and in Spain. Its name comes from a Latin word meaning "flowers of copper."

Chemical composition: $CuSO_4 \cdot 5H_2O$
Crystal system: Triclinic
Hardness: 2.5
Specific gravity: 2.3
Streak: Colorless to bluish-white

Chrysocolla

Chrysocolla is a minor ore of copper. It forms blue to blue-green crystals. Chrysocolla is soft and brittle, but it has been found mixed with quartz, which results in a much harder stone. A variety that contains malachite is found in Israel and can be used as an ornamental stone. Places where large masses are found include Arizona and New Mexico, in the United States, and Chile, Morocco, and Zimbabwe. The name comes from two Greek words meaning "gold glue," referring to its former use in soldering pieces of gold together.

Chemical composition: $Cu_2H_2Si_2O_5(OH)_4$
Crystal system: Monoclinic
Hardness: 2–4—**Specific gravity:** 2–2.4
Streak: White when pure

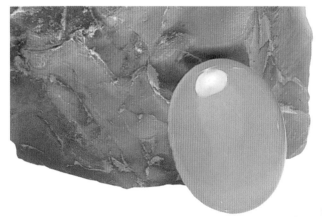

Cuprite

Cuprite is copper oxide. It is a major ore of copper and is found worldwide with other copper minerals, usually in dry regions. It most often occurs in large masses, but may form clear red crystals, which can be cut as gemstones. Sources of fine crystals include Chile, France, and Namibia. They are also found in the southwest United States, especially Arizona. The name comes from a Latin word meaning "copper."

Chemical composition: Cu_2O
Crystal system: Isometric
Hardness: 3.5–4
Specific gravity: 6.1
Streak: Brownish-red

Secondary Minerals

Descloizite

Descloizite is found in many parts of the world, but it is rare. It is an important ore of the metallic element vanadium, which is used to make very hard steel. Descloizite is found in the western United States and Mexico. Some of the most impressive crystals have been found in Namibia. Descloizite forms fine, orange to dark reddish-brown or green crystals. It is named for a French mineralogist from the 1800's, Alfred des Cloizeux.

Chemical composition: $Pb(Zn,Cu)(VO_4)(OH)$
Crystal system: Orthorhombic
Hardness: 3–3.5—Specific gravity: 6.2
Streak: Yellowish-orange to brownish-red

Fluorite

Fluorite may be colorless, white, yellow, green, blue, pink, purple, or black. Fluorite is common. It is found in limestone quarries and sometimes also in deposits of metal ore. One variety of fluorite, blue John, is only found in Derbyshire in England and has bands of violet and white. Major deposits of fluorite are found in Canada, England, Germany, Mexico, and the United States. The largest deposits in the United States are in Illinois and Kentucky. Some lenses in optical instruments are made of fluorite. Fluorite is also used to make hydrofluoric acid—a chemical required for making aluminum. Fluorite's name comes from a Latin word meaning "to flow," because of its use as a flux for separating melted metals from impurities.

Chemical composition: CaF_2
Crystal system: Isometric
Hardness: 4—Specific gravity: 3–3.2—Streak: White

Dioptase

Dioptase is a copper silicate; it is very popular with collectors because of its dark green, glassy crystals. It is found in the oxidized zone of copper deposits. The main sources include Arizona in the United States, Chile, the Democratic Republic of the Congo, Namibia, and Kazakhstan. A few crystals are cut to form gemstones. Its name comes from two Greek words, meaning "to see through."

Chemical composition: $CuSiO_2(OH)$
Crystal system: Rhombohedral
Hardness: 5—Specific gravity: 3.3–3.4—Streak: Green

Hemimorphite

Hemimorphite is an ore of zinc. It forms large masses and fibrous crusts in zinc ore deposits. It is usually white, but may also be yellow, green, or blue. The mineral's name—hemimorphite—refers to the fact that its crystals have different shapes at opposite ends. Because of this structure, heat or pressure can cause the opposite ends of a crystal to develop opposite electric charges. Good crystals come from Mexico. Other sources include Algeria, the United Kingdom, Germany, Italy, and the United States, especially the states of Colorado, Missouri, Montana, and New Jersey.

Chemical composition: $Zn_4Si_2O_7(OH)_2 \cdot H_2O$
Crystal system: Orthorhombic
Hardness: 4.5–5—Specific gravity: 3.4–3.5—Streak: Colorless

Smithsonite

Smithsonite is zinc carbonate. It is named for the chemist James Smithson, founder of the Smithsonian Institution in Washington, D.C. Smithsonite occurs as white, green, blue-green, pink, or yellow masses, or more rarely as crystals. It is found with other zinc ore deposits in such places as Greece, Mexico, and Namibia. United States sources include Arkansas, Colorado, and New Mexico. It is polished and used as an ornamental stone.

Chemical composition: $ZnCO_3$
Crystal system: Rhombohedral
Hardness: 4–4.5—Specific gravity: 4.3–4.4—Streak: White

Malachite

Malachite is one of the ores of copper. It usually occurs as a green crust on other copper minerals, or as masses. The rare crystals are bright to dark green, with a silky luster. It is found worldwide in copper deposits. Some of the largest deposits are found in the Ural Mountains of Russia and in Australia, Mexico, and southern and central Africa. The best-known United States deposits are in Arizona. Malachite is used as an ornamental stone. Its name comes from a Greek word that describes its color.

Chemical composition: $CU_2CO_3(OH)_2$
Crystal system: Monoclinic
Hardness: 3.5–4—Specific gravity: 3.9–4—Streak: Pale green

Secondary Minerals

Rhodochrosite

Rhodochrosite is manganese carbonate. It forms masses and, more rarely, crystals in shades of pink and red. Outstanding red crystals come from South Africa. Other major sources include Mexico, Peru, and Romania. Good crystal sources in the United States include Arkansas, Colorado, and Montana. It is used as an ornamental stone and as a gemstone. The name comes from two Greek words describing its color.

Chemical composition: $MnCO_3$
Crystal system: Rhombohedral
Hardness: 3.5–4—Specific gravity: 3.4–3.6—Streak: White

Rhodonite

Rhodonite is manganese iron magnesium silicate. It occurs as masses, when its rose-red to pink color is sometimes veined with black manganese oxides, and also as crystals. The finest crystals are found at Franklin, New Jersey, in the United States, and in Australia, Russia, and Sweden. Cut crystals are prized by collectors. Large masses are cut, shaped, and polished to make beads, tabletops, and other objects. The name comes from a Greek word meaning "rose."

Chemical composition: $(Mn,Fe,Mg)SiO_3$
Crystal system: Triclinic
Hardness: 5.5–6—Specific gravity: 3.5–3.7—Streak: Colorless

Serpentine

Serpentine is the name of a group of minerals in which magnesium is combined with silica. Some serpentine rocks have the appearance of snakeskin, which gives the minerals their group name. Serpentine is found all over the world in altered igneous rocks. It has a greasy feel, and most of its many varieties range from blue-green to yellow-green. Types of serpentine include bowenite, lizardite, and antigorite, all of which are used to make jewelry and decorative objects or building materials. Chrysotile, a fibrous form of asbestos, was used for soundproofing and insulation.

Chemical composition:
$Mg_3Si_2O_5(OH)$
Crystal system:
Monoclinic
Hardness: 2.5–5
Specific gravity: 2.5–2.6
Streak: White

Silver

Silver is one of the precious metals. It is found as wires or scales of pure silver, and also, though rarely, as crystals such as those from Kongsberg in Norway. Native silver (pure silver that occurs naturally) is rare. Some places to find it include Nevada and Michigan in the United States, Ontario in Canada, and Australia, Mexico, and Germany. It often occurs with other silver minerals, such as argentite. The leading producers of silver from any type of silver mineral are Mexico, Peru, the United States, Australia, and Chile. People have used silver in many ways for more than 6,000 years. The name comes from an Old English word for the metal.

**Chemical composition: Ag—Crystal system: Isometric
Hardness: 2.5–3—Specific gravity: 10.5—Streak: Silver-white**

Talc

Talc is a soft mineral. It is formed by the effects of heat and water on ultra-basic rocks or dolomites. It is found in many parts of the world and forms lumps that vary in color from white through green to gray. It has a greasy feel. It is ground up to make talcum powder and used in making paint, paper, and soap. Slabs of talc are used to line furnaces. A variety called soapstone has many industrial uses. The leading talc-producing nations are China, Finland, India, and the United States. The name comes from an Arabic word.

**Chemical composition: $Mg_3Si_4O_{10}(OH)_2$
Crystal system: Monoclinic, triclinic
Hardness: 1—Specific gravity: 2.7–2.8—Streak: White**

Sphalerite

Sphalerite consists of zinc and sulfur and is the main ore for zinc. It occurs worldwide with deposits of other sulfides (minerals containing sulfur and some type of metal). It is also found in sedimentary rocks, especially limestone. It occurs in many colors—red, brown, black, yellow, green, white, or even colorless. It gives off a rotten-egg odor when scratched. Major deposits occur in Mexico, eastern Europe, Spain, England, and the

United States. The name sphalerite comes from a Greek word meaning "treacherous," because this mineral can be mistaken for the lead ore galena, but it contains no lead.

**Chemical composition: ZnS
Crystal system: Isometric
Hardness: 3.5–4
Specific gravity: 3.9–4.1
Streak: Light brown**

Secondary Minerals

Vanadinite

Vanadinite is lead vanadate chloride. It is an ore of vanadium, a metal used to make very hard steel. Vanadinite occurs in dry regions as a result of the slow weathering that produces chemical changes in lead ore. Crystals may be orange-red, yellow, or brown. Sources of good crystals include Mexico, Morocco, South Africa, and the southwestern United States, especially Arizona. It is named for vanadium, which in turn was named for Vanadis, the Scandinavian goddess of beauty.

Chemical composition: $Pb5(VO_4)_3Cl$
Crystal system: Hexagonal
Hardness: 2.75–3
Specific gravity: 6.7–7.2
Streak: White or yellowish

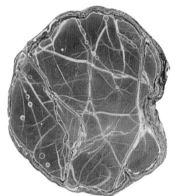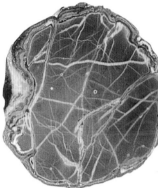

Variscite

Variscite is hydrated aluminum phosphate, and it is formed by water breaking down the minerals from igneous rocks such as pegmatite. Variscite is found in veins in the rock surrounding such igneous rocks. It forms as green nodules or lumps, but crystals are rare. Some of the best variscite crystals come from Utah and Arkansas in the United States. Its name comes from Variscia, the Roman name for the Vogtland region of Germany. The mineral is used ornamentally.

Chemical composition: $Al(PO_4)\cdot2H_2O$
Crystal system: Orthorhombic
Hardness: 3.5–4.5—Specific gravity: 2.2–2.8—Streak: White

Wulfenite

Wulfenite is lead molybdate. It is a minor ore of the element molybdenum, which has many industrial uses. It forms bright orange or red crystals, which are valued by collectors. Crystals may also be yellow or gray. Wulfenite is found with other lead and molybdenum deposits. It occurs throughout the southwestern United States, but the finest, deep orange-red crystals come from Arizona. There are other deposits in North Africa, Namibia, the Republic of the Congo, Iran, Mexico, Romania, and Australia. It is named for an Austrian mineralogist of the 1700's, Franz Xavier von Wulfen.

Chemical composition: $PbMoO_4$
Crystal system: Tetragonal
Hardness: 2.75–3—Specific gravity: 6.5–7—Streak: White

Calcite

Calcite has many industrial uses. Its name comes from the Latin word meaning "lime." Calcite occurs as clear or translucent crystals of various shapes. The crystals are usually colorless but may have pale tints. Calcite occurs all over the world and among all kinds of rocks. It makes up the largest part of limestone and marble. Golden-yellow crystals are found in Missouri, Kansas, and Oklahoma in the United States. The large clear crystals, known as Iceland spar, come from Iceland and have been used for making prisms.
Chemical composition: $CaCO_3$
Crystal system: Rhombohedral
Hardness: 3—Specific gravity: 2.7
Streak: White to pale gray

Pyrite

Pyrite is a compound of iron and sulfur. It is often called fool's gold because its cubic, brassy-yellow crystals can be mistaken for gold. Test the streak to tell the difference—gold's streak is golden-yellow; pyrite's is greenish-black. It occurs worldwide in many different environments. In the United States, fine crystals are found in Utah, Illinois, Pennsylvania, and Colorado. A mineral made up of similar elements, called marcasite, is used in jewelry. The name comes from the Greek word for fire, because pyrite sparks when struck with steel.
Chemical composition: FeS_2
Crystal system: Isometric
Hardness: 6–6.5—Specific gravity: 5.0–5.3
Streak: Greenish-black

Opal

Opal is a unique mineral because it does not form crystals. It is made up of regularly packed stacks of tiny silica spheres, which have a variety of different color effects. Opal's composition varies with the amount of water in it, and opal should not be allowed to get too dry. Variously colored opals are found in the western United States. The finest black opals and white opals come from Australia. Fine fire opals (transparent orange or red) and water opals (clear but with flashes of color) come from Mexico. The name is from a Sanskrit word meaning "precious stone."
Chemical composition: $SiO_2 \cdot H_2O$
Crystal system: None
Hardness: 5.5–6.5
Specific gravity: 2–2.2
Streak: don't try to test or you'll damage the stone

Quartz

Quartz is one of the hardest and most common minerals. Except for feldspar, it is the most common material in the crust of the earth's continents. It occurs all over the world as masses, and also as crystals, some of them huge. Pure quartz is colorless, but there are many colored varieties, including rose quartz (pink), amethyst (purple to violet), citrine (yellow to golden), and smoky quartz (pale brown to black). The tightly packed crystals of some quartz including agate, onyx, and chalcedony—can only be seen with a microscope. The name quartz comes from the German word for the mineral.
Chemical composition: SiO_2
Crystal system: Rhombohedral
Hardness: 7
Specific gravity: 2.65
Streak: White

Metamorphic Minerals

Anorthite

Anorthite is calcium aluminum silicate. It is found worldwide in many igneous and metamorphic rocks. Albite and anorthite are at opposite ends of the plagioclase series of feldspars. The other members of the series, which have decreasing amounts of sodium and increasing amounts of calcium, are oligoclase, andesine, labradorite, and bytownite. Anorthite's colorless, white, gray, or greenish crystals are uncommon, but places they occur include New Jersey and California in the United States and Italy and Japan. Its name comes from two Greek words meaning "not straight," which refers to the uneven way in which the crystal splits.

Chemical composition: $CaAl_2Si_2O_8$— **Crystal system: Triclinic**
Hardness: 6–6.5—Specific gravity: 2.7—Streak: White

Andalusite

Andalusite is aluminum silicate. It is found mainly in metamorphic rocks, especially gneisses, schists, and slates. Its color can be white, gray, pink, brown, or green. Andalusite is transparent or translucent. An opaque brown variety called chiastolite has light and dark sections that form a cross or checkered pattern. Places it is found include Australia and in the United States in California and Massachusetts. Good transparent crystals often come from Brazil or Sri Lanka. Andalusite is used to make ceramics. The finest crystals are cut as gemstones, including the beige, brown, or green material found in Brazil. It is named for Andalusia, the southern region of Spain, where it was once mined.

Chemical composition: Al_2SiO_5
Crystal system: Orthorhombic
Hardness: 6.5–7.5
Specific gravity: 3.1–3.2
Streak: Colorless

Albite

Albite is sodium aluminum silicate. It is one of the plagioclase series of feldspars, an important group of rock-forming minerals. It is part of many igneous and metamorphic rocks. Most albite is white, but specimens are found that are colored bluish, gray, reddish, or greenish. Albite is found worldwide, especially in granites, pegmatites, and igneous rocks. Its crystals are transparent or translucent. Places where good specimens are found include California and Virginia in the United States, and in Austria, Brazil, and Switzerland. In industry, albite is used in making ceramics. Its name comes from a Latin word meaning "white."

Chemical composition: $NaAlSi_3O_8$
Crystal system: Triclinic
Hardness: 6–6.5
Specific gravity: 2.6
Streak: Colorless

Axinite

Axinite contains aluminum, boron, calcium, and silica, with small amounts of iron and manganese. Places where it occurs include hydrothermal veins and areas of contact metamorphism where existing rock is altered by contact with hot volcanic intrusions. Its color varies from brown through olive-green, purple, and yellow. Some fine gem quality crystals come from California in the United States, and from Mexico, Japan, and France. The name comes from a Greek word meaning "ax," because axinite forms sharp, wedge-shaped crystals.

Chemical composition: $(Ca,Mn,Fe,Mg)_3Al_2BSi_4O_{15}(OH)$
Crystal system: Triclinic—Hardness: 6.5–7
Specific gravity: 3.3–3.4
Streak: Colorless or white

Diopside

Diopside is magnesium calcium silicate. It occurs mainly in metamorphosed limestone and dolomite in many parts of the world, including California and New York in the United States, Ontario and Quebec in Canada, and in Finland, Italy, and Russia. Diopside forms crystals varying in color from green to brown. Some of the finest of these are cut as gemstones. The name comes from Greek words meaning "two" and "appearance."

Chemical composition: $CaMgSi_2O_6$
Crystal system: Monoclinic
Hardness: 5–6
Specific gravity: 3.22–3.38
Streak: White, gray, or green

Corundum

Corundum is aluminum oxide, and it is the second hardest mineral after diamond. It comes in many colors. The colored crystals are valued as gemstones. Those called sapphires are found in shades of blue, yellow, pink, green, orange, violet, white, or black because they contain traces of iron, titanium, and other elements. Crystals that are deep red because of the presence of chromium are called rubies. The gemstones come from many countries: the finest rubies come from metamorphosed limestones in Myanmar, and the best sapphires are found in placer deposits in Sri Lanka. The name corundum comes from the Tamil name for ruby.

Chemical composition: Al_2O_3—Crystal system: Hexagonal
Hardness: 9—Specific gravity: 3.9–4.1—Streak: White

Metamorphic Minerals

All the minerals on this page are garnets, which occur as crystals in many different metamorphic rocks. Several types of garnet are used as gemstones.

Almandine

Almandine is iron aluminum silicate. It forms in such regional metamorphic rock as schist and gneiss—and in some contact metamorphic rock. Its crystals are deep blood-red or brownish-red. Fine crystals are found in many parts of the United States, especially Alaska and Idaho. Most gem-quality almandine comes from India and Sri Lanka, however. Some almandine that is not gem quality is ground finely to make sandpaper. Almandine is probably named for Alabanda, a town in southwest Turkey that was an early center for cutting these gems.

Chemical composition: $Fe_3Al_2(SiO_4)_3$
Crystal system: Isometric
Hardness: 6.5–7.5—Specific gravity: 4.3—Streak: White

Grossularite

Grossularite is calcium aluminum silicate; its color varies. Grossularite usually forms in contact metamorphic rock. The mineral's color may be white, yellow, green, orange-red, brown, or pink. Many crystals are used as gemstones, including stones from Italy, Kenya, Mexico, South Africa, and Tanzania. Sources for grossularite in the United States include New England and California. The name comes from the Latin word meaning "gooseberry," because some stones are the pale green color of the fruit.

Chemical composition: $Ca_3Al_2(SiO_4)_3$
Crystal system: Isometric
Hardness: 6.5–7
Specific gravity: 3.5–3.6
Streak: White

Pyrope

Pyrope is magnesium aluminum silicate. It is found in peridotites and serpentines, particularly in the diamond-bearing kimberlites of South Africa. Crystals are deep orange-red to purple-red. Most gem varieties come from India or East Africa. In the United States, pyrope is found in Arizona, New Mexico, North Carolina, and Utah. The name comes from a Greek word meaning "fire-eyed."

Chemical composition: $Mg_3Al_2(SiO_4)_3$
Crystal system: Isometric
Hardness: 7–7.5—Specific gravity: 3.5–3.8—Streak: White

Spessartite

Spessartite is manganese aluminum silicate and occurs in gneisses, schists, and granite pegmatites. Crystals are orange-red. Sources of fine crystals include California and Virginia in the United States, and Norway, Germany, Sri Lanka, and Brazil. It is named for the Spessart Mountains of Bavaria, Germany.

Chemical composition: $Mn_3Al_2(SiO_4)_3$
Crystal system: Isometric
Hardness: 7
Specific gravity: 3.8–4.2
Streak: White

Dumortierite

Dumortierite is a hard mineral found in metamorphic rocks containing aluminum. It is greenish-blue, pink, or violet and is translucent. The crystals are rare. Some crystals are transparent enough to be cut as gemstones. Dumortierite sources in the United States include Arizona, California, Nevada, and New York. Other countries where fine crystals have been found include Brazil and Namibia. Dumortierite is used to make the ceramic portion of spark plugs and heat-proof linings for furnaces. It is named for the French paleontologist of the 1800's, Eugene Dumortier.

Chemical composition: $Al_7(BO_3)(SiO_4)_3O_3$
Crystal system: Orthorhombic
Hardness: 7—Specific gravity: 3.3–3.4
Streak: White

Epidote

Epidote is calcium aluminum iron silicate—it is found in many metamorphic and igneous rocks. Epidote forms long needle-shaped crystals, green to brown in color. It is occasionally used as a gemstone but has no other commercial value. The best crystals come from Austria. In the United States, sources of epidote include Alaska and California. The name comes from a Greek word meaning "to increase."

Chemical composition: $Ca_2(Al,Fe)_3(SiO_4)_3(OH)$
Crystal system: Monoclinic
Hardness: 6–7
Specific gravity: 3.3–3.5
Streak: Colorless to gray

Graphite

Graphite is a soft mineral. It is pure carbon, like diamond, but formed under conditions of lower temperatures and less pressure, usually in metamorphosed rocks. Graphite is black or dark gray and flexible, with a greasy feel. Its most familiar use is as the "lead" in pencils, actually a mixture of graphite and clay. The name comes from the Greek word meaning "to write." Graphite forms large masses and six-sided crystals.

Chemical composition: C—Crystal system: Hexagonal
Hardness: 1.9–2.3—Specific gravity: 2.1
Streak: Black or dark gray

Kyanite

Kyanite, also spelled cyanite, is aluminum silicate and generally occurs in schists, gneisses, and granite pegmatites. It forms long blue or green crystals, which are sometimes used as gemstones. Locations with kyanite deposits include the United States, Australia, Brazil, Switzerland, and East Africa. The name comes from a Greek word meaning "blue."

Chemical composition: Al_2SiO_5—Crystal system: Triclinic
Hardness: 4–5 along the length of a crystal, 6–7 across it
Specific gravity: 3.5–3.7—Streak: Colorless

Metamorphic Minerals

Phlogopite

This name comes from a Greek word meaning "firelike," because its light brown to yellow crystals usually have a reddish tinge. It belongs to the mica group of minerals. It can occur as large six-sided crystals, which are often in metamorphosed limestones and dolomites. Some of the biggest crystals are found in Ontario and Quebec in Canada, in Madagascar, and in Sri Lanka. Phlogopite is used industrially as an electrical insulator.

Chemical composition: $KMg_3Si_3AlO_{10}(F,OH)_2$
Crystal system: Monoclinic
Hardness: 2–3—Specific gravity: 2.7–2.9—Streak: Colorless

Pyrophyllite

Pyrophyllite is an aluminum silicate. It rarely forms crystals. It occurs as large masses, with radiating, shell-like shapes. It varies in color from white through shades of gray and green to yellow, and it has a soapy feel. Large deposits have been found in Arkansas, California, Georgia, and the Carolinas in the United States. South Africa has an unusual black variety of pyrophyllite. The mineral has several industrial uses. Its name comes from two Greek words meaning "fire" and "leaf," because it flakes when heated.

Chemical composition: $Al_2Si_4O_{10}(OH)_2$
Crystal system: Monoclinic and triclinic
Hardness: 1–2
Specific gravity: 2.8–2.9
Streak: White

Scheelite

Scheelite is calcium tungstate. Its colorless to yellow, green, or brown crystals occur mainly in contact metamorphic deposits, but also in hydrothermal veins, pegmatites, and placer deposits. Scheelite is an important ore of tungsten, and economically important deposits occur in many places. It is named for the German-born Swedish chemist of the 1700's, Carl W. Scheele.

Chemical composition: $CaWO_4$—Crystal system: Tetragonal
Hardness: 4.5–5—Specific gravity: 5.9–6.1—Streak: White

Spinel

Spinel is magnesium aluminum oxide, and it is best known as a gemstone. Its crystals come in shades of red, blue, green, and brown to black. It is very hard. It is found worldwide in metamorphosed limestones and in placer deposits. Gem-quality crystals come mostly from Myanmar and Sri Lanka. In the United States, fine blue crystals come from Montana, and large crystals are found in New Jersey and New York. Its name refers to the shape of some of the crystals and comes from a Latin word meaning "thorn."

Chemical composition: $MgAl_2O_4$
Crystal system: Isometric
Hardness: 7.5–8
Specific gravity: 3.6–4
Streak: White

Staurolite

Staurolite is an iron aluminum silicate often with some magnesium or zinc. It is found in metamorphic rocks, including schists and gneisses. Its dark to yellowish-brown crystals often occur as twins, forming a cross up to 2 inches (5 centimeters) long. This is the origin of its name, which comes from a Greek word meaning "a cross." Places where good crystals are found include Georgia, New Mexico, North Carolina, and Virginia in the United States, and many countries, including Brazil and Switzerland. A very few transparent crystals may be cut as gemstones.

Chemical composition: $Fe_2Al_9O_6(SiO_4)_4(OH)_2$
Crystal system: Monoclinic
Hardness: 7–7.5—Specific gravity: 3.6–3.8—Streak: White

Vesuvianite

Vesuvianite is calcium magnesium aluminum silicate. It was first identified on the slopes of the Italian volcano, Mount Vesuvius, which is how it got its name. It is also called idocrase, from two Greek words meaning "a mixture of forms," because its prismlike crystals vary in shape. The colors vary, including yellow, green, reddish-brown, and blue. Californite is a translucent green to gray type of vesuvianite found mainly in California. Other important sources of vesuvianite include Vermont in the United States, Quebec in Canada, Kenya, Mexico, Norway, and Switzerland. Some of the transparent crystals may be cut as gemstones.

Chemical composition: $Ca_{10}Mg_2Al_4(SiO_4)_5(Si_2O_7)_2(OH)_4$
Crystal system: Tetragonal
Hardness: 6–7
Specific gravity: 3.3–3.5;
Streak: White

Wollastonite

Wollastonite is calcium silicate. It occurs in metamorphosed limestone. The mineral varies from colorless through white to very pale green. Some of the finest crystals come from New Jersey in the United States, Finland, and Romania. Other sources in the United States include California, New York, and Texas. Massive wollastonite deposits are found in northwest France, Germany, and Mexico. It is used in making heat-proof materials and is named for the English mineralogist of the 1700's, William H. Wollaston.

Chemical composition: $CaSiO_3$—Crystal system: Triclinic
Hardness: 4.5–5—Specific gravity: 2.87–3.1—Streak: White

Find Out More

Glossary

acid: any chemical compound with a sour taste; turns blue litmus paper red

aggregate: rock made from a mixture of mineral fragments

amorphous: crystal lacking a particular pattern or regular structure

atom: basic unit of a chemical element

batholith: huge underground mass of solidified igneous rock

carbonate: crystallized compound that includes a solidified form of carbonic acid (CO_3); example: siderite ($FeCO_3$)

cavity: hole in a rock mass, often lined with crystals

chloride: salt crystallized from hydrochloric acid

cleavage: line along which a crystal will easily break to form a flat surface

compound: mixture of two or more chemical elements

core: the name for the center of Earth

country rock: basic rock underlying an area of the landscape

crust: outer layer of Earth, on which we live

crystal: naturally occurring mineral with many flat surfaces

crystal systems: various shapes of crystals

deposit: vein, dike, or other mineral formation present in large quantities

dike: thin sheet of igneous rock, which forces its way as magma into a vertical crack in country rock

element, chemical: pure substance that contains only one kind of atom

erosion: wearing away of rocks by the action of wind or water

evaporation: process by which a liquid turns into a gas

feldspar: any one of a group of rock-forming silicate minerals

fossil: remains, impression, or cast of a once-living plant or animal found within rock

gem/gemstone: crystal that is cut and polished for display

geology: study of rocks and minerals

grain: very small fragment of a mineral

hexagonal: one of the crystal systems

humus: dark brown, powdery soil that forms when plants and the bodies of insects and other animals decay

hydrate: mineral composed of silica and a metallic element, combined with water

hydrothermal vein: crack in rock filled by new minerals that have formed from a solution of very hot water and existing minerals

igneous rock: rock formed from magma or lava when a volcano erupts

impurities: traces of various minerals in a substance

lava: molten or partly molten magma when it is thrown out by a volcano

magma: molten material in Earth's mantle or crust; it may solidify to form igneous rock

mantle: layer of molten rock under the crust and on which the continental plates float

mass: large, irregularly shaped lump of rock or mineral

metamorphic rock: any rock that has been altered by volcanic activity or the movement of continents

mica: any one of a group of minerals that splits in one direction into sheets

Mohs Scale: measurement system for hardness of crystals

molybdate: salt crystallized from an acid and containing molybdenum (Mo)

monoclinic: one of the crystal systems

native mineral: mineral made from only one element, such as gold (Au), silver (Ag), copper (Cu), platinum (Pt), or mercury (Hg)

nodule: small, rounded lump of a mineral or rock, usually found within a different type of rock

nugget: lump of metal, such as gold (Au)

opaque: cannot be seen through; opposite of transparent

ore: rock or mineral from which a metal or other mineral can be extracted in commercial quantities

orthorhombic: one of the crystal systems

oxide: crystallized compound of oxygen (O) with another element

oxidized: something that has combined with oxygen (O)

panning: mining technique

parent rock: igneous or sedimentary rock from which a metamorphic rock is made

pegmatite: very coarse-grained type of igneous rock, often found as dikes

phosphate: crystallized compound of phosphorus (P) with other elements

placer: deposit of sand or gravel in or near a river; it can contain gold (Au), platinum (Pt), or other heavy minerals

plagioclase: any one of a group of feldspars that contains both sodium (Na) and calcium (Ca)

plate, continental: section of Earth's crust and upper mantle that moves about, carrying the continents

precious metal: gold (Au), silver (Ag), platinum (Pt), or other rare metals

pyroxene: any one of a group of silicate minerals; their chemical formulas do not contain water (H_2O)

quartz: common group of rock-forming silicate minerals

secondary mineral: mineral found in the ore of another mineral

sediment: tiny piece of rock, weathered by wind or water, which makes up sedimentary rock

sedimentary rock: rock made from layer upon layer of mud, sand, and plant and animal remains, which have been compressed together deep underground, often under the sea

sheet: flat plate of a mineral that has formed horizontally between two layers of country rock

silicate: large group of minerals that do not dissolve in acid and always contain the elements silicon (Si) and oxygen (O)

sill: sheetlike body of igneous rock, typically lying horizontally between layers of country rock

solution: mixture of something dissolved in a liquid

specific gravity: test to identify a mineral

stalactite: downward-growing column formed by dripping water containing a solution of limestone; may join with a stalagmite to make a pillar

stalagmite: upward-rising column of limestone, formed from the drip of a stalactite

streak: true color of a mineral, used for identification

sulfate: salt crystallized from sulfuric acid

sulfide: compound of sulfur (S) and other elements

tetragonal: one of the crystal systems

transparent: describes something, such as plain glass, that can be seen through

triclinic: one of the crystal systems

trigonal: one of the crystal systems

tungstate: salt crystallized from an acid containing tungsten (W)

ultra-basic: rock, such as dolomite, containing little or no quartz or feldspars; made mainly of iron (Fe) and magnesium (Mg)

variety: mineral that has had another mineral or element mixed into it, producing a slightly different chemical result—for example: a blue variety of pectolite called Larimar

vein: vertical deposit of mineral that has seeped into a crack in country rock as a solution

Organizations

The **American Federation of Mineralogical Societies** is a hobby- and education-oriented group dedicated to the study and appreciation of earth science; it publishes the *American Federation Newsletter*. Contact: AFMS Central Office, P.O. Box 302, Glyndon, Maryland 21071-0302; (410) 833-7926.
http://www.amfed.org

The **Geological Society of America** caters primarily to professional and academic geologists, but it can be a helpful contact for amateurs as well. Contact: Geological Society of America, P.O. Box 9140, Boulder, Colorado 80301-9140; (303) 447-2020.
http://www.geosociety.org

In Canada, the **Geological Survey of Canada** is your best starting point. Contact: Geological Survey of Canada, National Resources Canada, Earth Sciences Section, 601 Booth Street, Ottawa, Ontario K1A OE8; (613) 996-3919.
http://gsc.nrcan.gc.ca/index_e.php

The **Mineralogical Society of America** also caters primarily to professional and academic geologists. Contact: Mineralogical Society of America, 3635 Concorde Parkway, Suite 500, Chantilly, Virginia 20151-1125; (703) 652-9950.
http://www.minsocam.org

The **U.S. Geological Survey** is a terrific storehouse of information, including maps and guides. For additional information, contact: Earth Science Information Center, 12201 Sunrise Valley Drive, Reston, Virginia 20192; (888) 275-8747.
http://www.usgs.gov or http://ask.usgs.gov

Index

Additional Resources

Earth Treasures: Where to Collect Minerals, Rocks & Fossils in the United States (4 volumes). Allan W. Eckert (iUniverse, 2000).

A Field Guide to Rocks and Minerals Frederick H. Pough (Houghton Mifflin, 1998) and ***The Peterson First Guide to Rocks and Minerals*** (1991).

Guide to Minerals, Rocks and Fossils A. C. Bishop, William R. Hamilton, and Alan R. Woolley (Firefly Books, 2005).

Handbook of Rocks, Minerals and Gemstones Walter Schumann (Houghton Mifflin, 1993).

National Audubon Society First Field Guide: Rocks and Minerals Edward R. Ricciuti and Margaret W. Carruthers (Scholastic, 1998).

Rocks, Gems, and Minerals Trudi S. Trueit (Franklin Watts, 2003).

Index